Instructor's Manual and Test-Item File

Merriman's

A History of Modern Europe

Instructor's Manual and Test-Item File

Merriman's
A History of Modern Europe

Michael D. Bess
VANDERBILT UNIVERSITY

W. W. NORTON & COMPANY
New York • London

The text of this book is composed in Bembo.
Composition and book design by David Budmen, Willow Graphics, Woodstown, N.J.

Cover illustration: *The Harbour of Middelburg*, c. 1625, by Adriaen van der Venne.
Rijksmuseum, Amsterdam.

ISBN 0-393-96887-1 (pbk.)

W. W. Norton & Company, Inc., 500 Fifth Avenue, New York, N.Y. 10110
   http: // web.wwnorton.com
W. W. Norton & Company Ltd., 10 Coptic Street, London WCIA IPU

Contents

Preface

I have written this manual as an aid both to new instructors and to more seasoned teachers who seek new ideas for lectures or examinations. Each chapter starts with a detailed outline of the corresponding chapter in John Merriman's text. I then offer suggestions for possible lecture topics on the chapter's main subjects, including a list of books or primary source documents that provide fertile material for lectures, as well as possible films or slide show topics that make good accompaniment to the standard lecture format. Test materials follow: a series of ten multiple-choice questions, a series of short-answer essay questions (designed to elicit interpretive, critical reflection from undergraduate students), a series of ten true/false questions, and finally a series of ten major events from the period discussed in the chapter, to be placed in chronological order by the students.

I would like to thank John Merriman for writing this superb (and much-needed) textbook, as well as Jon Durbin, Steve Forman, Tim Holahan, and Linda Puckette at Norton, for giving me the opportunity to write this instructor's manual, and for the good cheer and professionalism with which they offered assistance and guidance to me throughout the project.

MICHAEL D. BESS
VANDERBILT UNIVERSITY

Part One
Foundations

Chapter 1
Medieval Legacies and Transforming Discoveries

This chapter provides an overview of the major characteristics—social, economic, and cultural—of European society around the year 1500. It also details the principal agencies of change that transformed Europe from a medieval society to an emerging early-modern one.

Chapter Outline

I. A period of profound change
    A. Discoverers and rebels
    B. Demographic shifts and commerce
    C. State-building
    D. New technologies and their impact

II. Medieval roots of modern European society
    A. Political and cultural fragmentation
        1. Invaders from afar
        2. Varieties of overlapping authority and sovereignty
        3. The importance of local loyalties
        4. Religious divisions
        5. Tensions between Church and State
        6. Conflict with the Islamic world
        7. Roman law, canon law, and common law
        8. Linguistic boundaries
    B. The structure of medieval society
        1. Clergy
        2. Nobility
        3. Peasantry
    C. Feudalism
        1. Mutual bonds

  2. A lopsided power relationship
  3. The impact of the Black Death
 D. An agricultural economy
  1. Primitive farming methods
  2. Contrasts between Eastern and Western Europe
  3. Migrant labor
  4. The spread of a cash economy
 E. The intertwining of religion and popular culture
  1. A factor permeating every aspect of life
  2. Moral authority
  3. Belief in the supernatural

III. The physiognomy of an emerging modernity
 A. New demographic patterns
  1. Diseases and famines
  2. Short life expectancy
  3. Marriage and the slow rise in population
 B. Economic growth
  1. The emergence of new banking practices
  2. The commercial boom of the sixteenth century
  3. New products, new means of distribution and transport
  4. The guild system
 C. The importance of towns
  1. Administration
  2. Trade
  3. Learning
  4. Municipal liberties and the seeds of a democratic impulse
 D. The emergence of sovereign states
  1. Medieval roots
  2. The primacy of kings over noble rivals
  3. Centralization in France and Britain
  4. The failure of consolidation in the Holy Roman Empire
  5. The growth of bureaucratic government
  6. Limits to state authority

IV. The impact of new technologies and discoveries
 A. Gunpowder and the transformation of warfare
  1. Muskets
  2. Artillery
  3. Mercenaries and conscription
 B. Printing

        1.   The spread of a new technology
        2.   Rising literacy
   C. Overseas exploration
        1.   Rivalry between Spain and Portugal
        2.   Columbus
        3.   New trade routes by sea
        4.   Conquering the Americas
        5.   The decimation caused by European diseases
        6.   Exchanging new crops across the ocean
        7.   Colonization and slavery

V.   Three currents of change that brought the Middle Ages to an end
   A. The Renaissance
   B. The opening of the New World
   C. The Reformation

Suggestions for Lecture Topics

For a lecture on the meanings of "nationhood" see Benedict Anderson, *Imagined Communities.*

For a lecture on the everyday life of Europeans during the early-modern period, see Georges Duby, ed., *A History of Private Life.*

An excellent source for a more in-depth lecture on the "texture" of life for common people in Europe is Emmanuel Le Roy Ladurie, *Montaillou: The Promised Land of Error.*

A splendid film to show students on this period, rich in its historical evocation and providing an excellent starting point for class discussion, is *The Return of Martin Guerre.*

For a lecture on women in this transitional period, see Edith Ennen, *The Medieval Woman.*

William McNeill's book, *Plagues and Peoples,* makes a useful source on the Black Death and its far-reaching impact; this is a subject that many undergraduates find fascinating.

Multiple-Choice Questions

1. Gunpowder was invented in
   a.   Japan.

    b.   Italy.
    c.   Britain.
    d.   China.
    e.   none of the above

Answer: d

2. The Black Death, or bubonic plague, killed approximately what percentage of the European population during the fourteenth century?
    a.   between 5 percent and 10 percent
    b.   between 10 percent and 20 percent
    c.   between 20 percent and 30 percent
    d.   between 30 percent and 50 percent
    e.   between 50 percent and 80 percent

Answer: d

3. In early-modern European society, the following legal forms existed:
    a.   canon law, common law, and tort law
    b.   common law, Greek law, and Roman law
    c.   tort law and canon law
    d.   Roman law, canon law, and common law
    e.   Islamic law, Christian law, and Jewish law

Answer: d

4. The phrase "municipal liberties" refers primarily to
    a.   the freedom of city dwellers to choose their own religious faith.
    b.   the freedom of city dwellers to engage in commerce.
    c.   the freedom of cities from legal duties to, and taxation by, surrounding nobles and the Church.
    d.   the freedom of cities to wage war on other cities.
    e.   none of the above

Answer: c

5. The three principal legal and social divisions within medieval society were
    a.   clergy, nobility, and peasantry.
    b.   rich, poor, and clergy.
    c.   Catholics, Protestants, and Jews.
    d.   king, clergy, and peasantry.
    e.   bourgeoisie, proletariat, and nobility.

Answer: a

6. The two European nations that first embarked on overseas exploration and colonization were
   a. Italy and Britain.
   b. Spain and Germany.
   c. France and Britain.
   d. Italy and Spain.
   e. Spain and Portugal.

Answer: e

7. Which of the following statements most accurately describes the impact of the development of gunpowder on Europe's nobility?
   a. Gunpowder had little effect on European warfare because early weapons were so primitive as to be virtually useless.
   b. Gunpowder led to the end of knights in armor and jousting with lances.
   c. Gunpowder allowed kings to wage war against the nobles and subdue them.
   d. Gunpowder was so scarce and expensive that only the nobles could afford to use it.
   e. none of the above

Answer: b

8. What was the impact of new printing technologies on European society?
   a. rising literacy rates
   b. cheaper books
   c. stricter censorship laws
   d. the emergence of Latin as a universal language
   e. both a and b

Answer: e

9. Which of the following did the European conquistadors NOT bring with them to the New World?
   a. pigs
   b. horses
   c. smallpox
   d. tomatoes
   e. sheep

Answer: d

10. Crop rotation was used primarily to

a. allow the fields to recover their fertility.
b. obey religious restrictions on diet.
c. follow the natural fertility cycles of the seasons.
d. none of the above
e. all of the above

Answer: a

Short-Answer Questions

1. What social and cultural forms are generally associated with the word "feudalism"?
2. Describe the role(s) played by religion in the lives of Europeans during the period around 1500.
3. What kinds of factors led to the waning of the Middle Ages and the emergence of a new, "early-modern" period of history?
4. Describe the role played by gunpowder in transforming warfare.
5. What were the Europeans seeking when they embarked on their voyages of discovery and exploration overseas? What did they find?
6. Describe the process by which centralized, sovereign states emerged from among the hodgepodge of smaller, fragmented polities of the Middle Ages.

True/False Questions

1. Compared to other areas of the world, Europe was racially and ethnically homogeneous.

Answer: F

2. The conflict with the Islamic world constituted one of the central features of European life during the years of transition from the medieval to the early-modern period.

Answer: T

3. Although a majority of the European clergy came from humble social roots, the majority of bishops and other Church leaders came from the nobility.

Answer: T

4. Migrant labor constituted a major part of the European economy around the year 1500.

Answer: T

5. Diseases and famines had been rooted out by the year 1500, causing a marked increase in population growth.

Answer: F

6. Many Europeans still believed in the supernatural around the year 1500.

Answer: T

7. The Holy Roman Empire was one of Europe's first successfully centralized states.

Answer: F

8. The printing press took many centuries to make any impact on European culture, because paper was not invented until the seventeenth century.

Answer: F

9. Columbus brought slaves back from the Americas when he returned to Spain.

Answer: F

10. Diseases carried by Europeans killed as many, if not more, people in the New World than the worst depredations of the conquistadors.

Answer: T

Chronology

Place the following items in correct chronological order.

8. Columbus' first voyage to the New World
3. Mongol invasions of Europe
7. Turks capture Constantinople
9. Venice establishes the first "ghetto" for Jews
5. Black Death ravages Europe
4. Marco Polo travels to China
2. Signing of Magna Carta
1. Holy Roman Empire founded
10. Ferdinand Magellan killed by Pacific islanders
6. Printing press with movable type invented

Chapter 2
The Renaissance

This chapter describes the cultural and artistic efflorescence of the Italian Renaissance, providing a detailed analysis of the underlying social and economic conditions that rendered this "rebirth" possible.

Chapter Outline

I.   Renaissance or "rebirth"
    A.   The rediscovery and revalorization of classical texts

II. Italy's city-states
    A.   Economic prosperity
        1.   Italy's role in East-West trade
        2.   The role of Roman law
        3.   Advanced transportation links
    B.   Florence, capitalist city
    C.   Venice and Genoa, rivals on the seas
    D.   Social structure
        1.   Popolo grasso
        2.   Mediocri
        3.   Popolo minuto
    E.   Politics in the city-states
        1.   Constitutional oligarchy
        2.   Hereditary despotism
        3.   The Venetian Republic
    F.   The condottieri
    G.   Inter-city diplomacy
    H.   The case of Florence
        1.   The fifth-largest city in Europe in the fourteenth century
        2.   A broad social hierarchy
        3.   The primacy of the Medici family

III. The spirit of the Renaissance
   A. Return to classicism
      1. Petrarch
      2. The impact of printing
   B. The new humanism
      1. Turning away from scholasticism
      2. The "art of living"
      3. Civic virtues
   C. The strong imprint of religion
      1. The Aeneid as allegory for pilgrimage of the Christian soul
   D. Secular wisdom from the classical texts
      1. The central notion of human individuality
      2. The idea of a "universal person"
      3. The prodigious curiosity of Leonardo da Vinci
   E. The world of women
      1. Strict subordination to men

IV. Renaissance art
   A. Architecture
      1. The influence of antiquity
   B. The key role of patronage
   C. Artists and the apprenticeship system
   D. Painting and sculpture
      1. The impact of neo-Platonism
      2. Naturalism
      3. Realistic depiction and perspective
   E. The High Renaissance
      1. Mannerism

V. The end of the Renaissance
   A. Economic decline saps the material base of the Renaissance
      1. Turkish incursions
      2. Competition from the French, English, Spanish, and Dutch
   B. Invasions and civil strife
      1. The French invasion of 1494 and Savonarola's virtual control of Florence
      2. The French invasion of 1499
      3. Machiavelli's plea for unity
      4. Expanding Spanish influence after 1530

Suggestions for Lecture Topics

The lives of individual Renaissance masters, such as Leonardo, Michelangelo, or Raphael, make fascinating material for brief vignettes within lectures. See the classic contemporary account by Giorgio Vasari on this subject.

A slide show of major Renaissance works is highly recommended for this chapter topic. Particularly effective is a side-by-side configuration of slides, in which students are encouraged to point out the contrasts between Renaissance and medieval works, and the points of similarity between Renaissance and classical works.

A lecture on Machiavelli is useful, since he remains highly influential to this day. Readings from *The Prince* can be taken as starting points for class discussion.

For the everyday lives of Renaissance courtiers, see *The Courtier* by Baldassare Castiglione.

For a lecture on Florence, see the excellent account by Gene Brucker, *Renaissance Florence*.

Multiple-Choice Questions

1. The word "Renaissance" means
   a. rebirth.
   b. mastery.
   c. flowering.
   d. resurgence.
   e. return.

Answer: a

2. Florence built up its prosperity particularly through
   a. farming.
   b. banking and textiles.
   c. trade and printing.
   d. conquest.
   e. both a and c

Answer: b

3. The main ruling noble house in Florence during the Renaissance was
   a. the Sforza family.

   b.   the Gonzaga family.
   c.   the Este family.
   d.   the Vinci family.
   e.   none of the above

Answer: e

4. The notion of "Renaissance humanism" refers to
   a.   a more charitable morality than that of the medieval period.
   b.   a total rejection of religion.
   c.   a belief that humans were superior to all other animals.
   d.   a renewed emphasis on human individuality in art and civic culture.
   e.   none of the above

Answer: d

5. Renaissance philosophers felt that classical antiquity
   a.   was a golden age.
   b.   should be emulated and improved upon by modern people.
   c.   was superior in art but inferior in socioeconomic organization.
   d.   both a and b
   e.   all of the above

Answer: d

6. Leonardo da Vinci was NOT a
   a.   painter.
   b.   poet.
   c.   sculptor.
   d.   designer of military weapons.
   e.   student of anatomy.

Answer: b

7. By the early 1500s the city-states of Italy
   a.   had formed an effective alliance among themselves.
   b.   had divided into two hostile alliances.
   c.   had divided into three hostile alliances.
   d.   had fallen under foreign domination.
   e.   none of the above

Answer: d

8. Venice and Genoa were primarily
   a.   sea powers and rivals.

    b.   land powers and rivals.
    c.   sea powers and allies.
    d.   land powers and allies.
    e.   none of the above

Answer: a

9. Machiavelli's ideal prince combined the qualities of
    a.   cunning and force.
    b.   kindness and foresightedness.
    c.   generosity and courage.
    d.   intelligence and religious piety.
    e.   artistic talent as well as administrative ability.

Answer: a

10. Girolamo Savonarola was:
    a.   a minstrel
    b.   a poet
    c.   a monk
    d.   an artisan
    e.   a historian

Answer: c

Short-Answer Questions

1. How important was the economic condition of the Italian city-states as a precondition for the Renaissance? Explain.
2. Briefly describe which were the principal Italian city-states during the Renaissance, and sketch a map of their geographical location.
3. Why were the philosophers of the Renaissance so strongly attracted to classical antiquity, and why did they refer to the Middle Ages as the "Dark Ages"?
4. Describe the contrast between humanism and scholasticism, as it was understood by Renaissance thinkers.
5. What kinds of factors caused the Renaissance to come to an end?

True/False Questions

1. Some Italian city-states were pioneering exemplars of modern democratic politics.

Answer: F

2. Rome is the city most frequently associated with the Renaissance.

Answer: F

3. The Medici family ruled Florence for much of the thirteenth century.

Answer: F

4. The High Renaissance is generally acknowledged among scholars as a more advanced and sophisticated phase in the history of art and culture than the Renaissance itself.

Answer: F

5. Donatello was a famous sculptor.

Answer: T

6. By the early 1500s, the economic center of gravity in Europe was shifting away from the Mediterranean and toward the Atlantic seaboard.

Answer: T

7. Baldassare Castiglione believed that a true courtier could not be taught to act properly, but had to be born with the requisite noble instincts.

Answer: F

8. Contrary to popular belief, much of Michelangelo's Sistine Chapel was in fact painted by the young Raphael.

Answer: F

9. Leonardo da Vinci died in France.

Answer: T

10. Niccolò Machiavelli was assassinated by emissaries of the pope.

Answer: F

Chronology

Place the following items in correct chronological order.

2. Cosimo de' Medici gains control of Florence
9. Niccolò Machiavelli publishes *The Prince*
10. Sack of Rome by troops of Charles V
5. Pazzi conspiracy in Florence
8. Michelangelo paints Sistine Chapel ceiling
3. Ottoman conquest of Constantinople
4. Peace of Lodi signed
6. Charles VIII invades Italy
1. "Babylonian Captivity" of the papacy
7. Savonarola burned for heresy

Chapter 3
The Two Reformations

This chapter sets forth the origins, causes, and general character of the Protestant Reformation. It details the legacy of the Northern Renaissance, the emerging criticism of Catholic abuses, and the social background of the reformers. Finally, it traces the course of the Reformation in its principal national settings and describes the Catholic reaction.

Chapter Outline

I. Emerging divisions within the Christian faith
    A. Catholic majorities
        1. Spain, France, Austria, Poland
        2. The Italian states, Bavaria, and southern Germany
    B. Protestant majorities
        1. England, the Dutch Netherlands, Scandinavia
        2. The northern German states, parts of Switzerland

II. The Northern Renaissance
    A. Humanism spreads northward
        1. The seminal role of the Dutch Netherlands
        2. Latin as an international language of high culture
        3. An emerging critical spirit
    B. Erasmus of Rotterdam
        1. Criticizing the established church institutions

III. Roots of the Reformation
    A. The growth of sovereign states and the erosion of papal authority
        1. The rise of national churches in France, Spain, and England
        2. The papal bull *Unam Sanctam* (1302)
        3. The "Avignon Papacy" (1305–1378)
        4. The Great Schism (1378–1417)

    B. Heretical and spiritual movements
1. Occam vs. Aquinas
2. "Nominalists": an emphasis on individual piety
3. Wyclif's de-emphasis on ritual, and the Lollard rebellion
    C. Conciliarism
1. The Council of Constance (1414–1418)
2. Subordinating papal authority to control by councils
    D. Clerical abuses
1. Indulgences: purchasing lesser punishment for sins
2. Sale of Church offices
3. Moral abuses
4. Exemption from taxation and civil justice
    E. Martin Luther
1. A scrupulous conscience
2. The influence of Nominalism
3. The 95 Theses: October 31, 1517
4. A new doctrine: "Faith alone brings salvation, not good works."
5. The Diet of Worms (1521)

IV. The social background of the Reformation
    A. An urban phenomenon at the outset
    B. The reform spreads among the middle and lower classes
    C. The peasant revolt (1525–1526)
1. Calls for social reform to accompany religious reform
2. The rebels crushed, with Luther's approval

V. The Reformation spreads
    A. The Lutheran Church is born
    B. Charles V confronts the Protestant Schmalkaldic League
    C. The Peace of Augsburg (1555)
1. *Cuius regio, eius religio*: the principle of state religion

VI. The Reformation in Switzerland and France
    A. Zwingli's reforms in Zurich
1. Sacraments: actual or symbolic transubstantiation?
    B. Anabaptist communities
1. Münster as the "New Jerusalem"
2. Mennonites
    C. Calvin
1. A deep-running anxiety
2. Rejecting the institution of penance

3. Not reconciliation with God, but obedience
4. Predestination
5. Calvin's transformation of Geneva after 1540
6. Huguenots in France, despite persecution
7. Dutch Calvinists fight for independence from Spain

VII. The English Reformation
   A. A royal divorce: Henry VIII and Catherine of Aragon
   B. The Act of Supremacy (1534): Church subordinated to royal authority
       1. The dissolution of the monasteries

VIII. The Catholic response: Counter-Reformation
   A. The Inquisition
   B. Loyola and the Society of Jesus: crusaders of the Counter-Reformation
       1. Missionaries and pamphlets
   C. The Council of Trent: reaffirming Church authority
   D. Catholic reformers
       1. Reaching out to the poor
       2. Teresa of Avila's mystical Catholicism

IX. Reformation Culture
   A. The Baroque style: inspiring awe in the viewer
   B. Printed pamphlets as part of a broader diffusion of written works
       1. Rising levels of literacy and education
   C. Popular festivals in a time of religious tensions
   D. Protestantism and women
       1. Subordination of women continued
       2. Revalorization of the family
       3. Witch hunts
   E. The legacy of the Reformation
       1. A revitalization of religion
       2. Secularization of government in Protestant states

Suggestions for Lecture Topics

Direct quotations from Martin Luther's own works make excellent material for a vivid introduction to the grievances and philosophical points that characterized the Reformation. A good book on Luther is Gerhard Brendler, *Martin Luther: Theology and Revolution.*

A "class debate" format, in which some defend the Catholic position while others defend the Protestant position, leads to lively exchanges between students and renders the underlying issues involved more accessible.

To make a link between this topic and more contemporary issues, a lecture on Max Weber's *Protestant Ethic and the Spirit of Capitalism* makes for an absorbing discussion.

For a lecture on Calvin, see William Bouwsma, *John Calvin: A Sixteenth-Century Portrait*.

For a lecture on the English Reformation, see Richard Rex, *Henry VIII and the English Reformation*. See also Richard Marius, *Thomas More*, for a biography of this fascinating figure.

Multiple-Choice Questions

1. Which of the following groups of nations had Catholic majorities?
   a. Spain, France, Austria, Poland
   b. France, Italy, Germany, England
   c. Austria, the Netherlands, Italy
   d. Spain, England, and Austria
   e. France, Italy, Scandinavia, Switzerland, Spain

Answer: a

2. Which of the following regions of the German states had Protestant majorities?
   a. northern Germany
   b. southern Germany
   c. both northern and southern Germany
   d. neither northern nor southern Germany

Answer: a

3. The international language of culture during the Reformation was
   a. French.
   b. Latin.
   c. Greek.
   d. Italian.
   e. none of the above

Answer: b

4. Erasmus of Rotterdam
   a. was a staunch defender of Catholic orthodoxy.

    b.   became a highly radical critic of Catholic orthodoxy.

    c.   was a moderate critic of Catholic orthodoxy.

    d.   was a Jew, and hence unaffected by the Reformation.

    e.   none of the above

Answer: c

5. The papal bull *Unam Sanctam*
    a.   defended the literal meaning of transubstantiation.
    b.   defended the selling of indulgences.
    c.   reasserted papal infallibility against Jews who questioned it.
    d.   excommunicated Martin Luther.
    e.   reasserted papal authority over all monarchs.

Answer: e

6. Martin Luther believed that:
    a.   good works and repentance would bring salvation.
    b.   God had predestined certain people for salvation before birth.
    c.   the Catholic Church was guilty of 95 sins.
    d.   faith alone, and not good works, would bring salvation.
    e.   the Catholic Church was capable of reforming itself.

Answer: d

7. The principle of *Cuius regio, eius religio* meant that
    a.   the religion of a ruler became the religion of his or her subjects.
    b.   no prince could have a different religion than the king.
    c.   every individual should be free to determine his or her own religion.
    d.   all Europeans should strive to unite under a single Christianity.
    e.   none of the above

Answer: a

8. The Anabaptists in Münster
    a.   believed that the end of the world was near.
    b.   believed that baptism was wrong.
    c.   believed in predestination.
    d.   both a and b
    e.   none of the above

Answer: a

9. King Henry VIII had how many wives during his life?
    a.   three

    b.   five
    c.   seven
    d.   eight
    e.   none of the above

Answer: e

10. Ignatius Loyola founded
    a.   the Capuchins.
    b.   the Ignatians.
    c.   the Jesuits.
    d.   the Jacobins.
    e.   all of the above

Answer: c

Short-Answer Questions

1. By the year 1600, which nations and regions of Europe had become predominantly Protestant, and which ones had remained predominantly Catholic?
2. What were the principal grievances and philosophical arguments put forward by the Protestant reformers against the Catholic Church?
3. In what ways did Calvinist Protestantism differ from Lutheran Protestantism?
4. What reasons did Henry VIII have for launching the Reformation in England?
5. How did the Catholic Church respond to the Reformation? Explain the actions it took.

True/False Questions

1. The attempt to create an "Avignon Papacy" was crushed by military force.

Answer: F

2. Conciliarism represented an attempt to undermine the absolute power of the pope.

Answer: T

3. Nominalists sought to re-emphasize the role of individual piety in the practice of the Christian faith.

Answer: T

4. At the Diet of Worms, Martin Luther compromised with the Catholic emissaries.

Answer: F

5. Martin Luther was hostile to the peasant revolt of 1525–1526.

Answer: T

6. Zwingli was a Swiss reformer.

Answer: T

7. The Act of Supremacy asserted the right of King Henry VIII to head the Church of England.

Answer: T

8. Teresa of Avila was a nun who converted to Protestantism after meeting Martin Luther.

Answer: F

9. The doctrine of predestination held that God had already decided, before one's birth, whether one would go to heaven or not, and that no number of good deeds in one's lifetime could change this.

Answer: T

10. Some popes and Catholic priests had concubines and children.

Answer: T

Chronology

Place the following items in correct chronological order.
    9. The first year of Calvin's rule in Geneva
    1. The papal bull *Unam Sanctam*
    7. The British Act of Supremacy
    3. The Council of Constance
    6. The German peasant revolt

  4. Luther's nailing of the 95 theses
 10. The Peace of Augsburg
  5. The Diet of Worms
  2. The "Avignon Papacy"
  8. The Anabaptist takeover of Münster

Chapter 4
The Wars of Religion

This chapter describes the religious divisions that brought bloodshed and devastation to France and the German states during the sixteenth and seventeenth centuries.

Chapter Outline

I. Religious antagonisms lead to war
    A. A patchwork of religious allegiances in the German states
    B. A religious civil war in France
    C. Long-term consequences: strengthening the institutions of monarchy

II. Catholics versus Huguenots in France
    A. Francis I consolidates the Valois monarchy
    B. The Concordat of Bologna (1516) reduces Catholic Church authority
    C. Economic crisis
        1. Inflation
        2. Diminishing agricultural efficiency for the peasantry
        3. Taxes and tithes
    D. French Calvinism slowly spreads in the 1500s
        1. The Treaty of Cateau-Cambrésis (1559): a Franco-Spanish truce
        2. Forty percent of the French nobility convert to Calvinism
    E. The regency of Catherine de Medici
        1. The Catholic Guise and Montmorency families
        2. The Huguenot Bourbon family
        3. Growing religious violence and polarization
    F. A series of religious wars during the 1560s
    G. The St. Bartholomew's Day Massacre of Huguenots (1572)
    H. The Catholic League vs. Henry of Navarre
        1. Henry's religious tergiversations
        2. Henry's military victory against the Catholic League (1587)

        3.   The "Day of Barricades" in Paris (1588)
        4.   Henry III assassinates the Duke of Guise (1588)
        5.   Henry of Navarre becomes Henry IV, a Catholic king (1593)
        6.   Final capitulation of the Catholic League (1598)

  I. Henry IV as monarch
        1.   Tightening the fiscal administration
        2.   The influence of the duke of Sully
        3.   The Edict of Nantes (1598): a compromise solution
        4.   Patronage of the arts
        5.   Swashbuckling ways
        6.   Encouraging manufacturing industries
        7.   Settlers for the New World
        8.   Assassination by a monk (1610)

  J. Louis XIII's reign
        1.   The influence of Cardinal Richelieu
        2.   Further centralization of royal power
        3.   Intendants for France's thirty-two districts
        4.   Turning against Catholic powers in the Thirty Years' War

III. The Thirty Years' War (1618–1648)
  A. The Holy Roman Empire's patchwork of a thousand states
        1.   Noncontiguous borders
        2.   Religious rivalries
  B. Origins of the Thirty Years' War
        1.   Rudolf II's failed crusade against Protestantism
        2.   Declining authority and power of the Empire
        3.   Tensions between Lutherans and Catholics
        4.   Growing Catholic-Protestant intolerance
        5.   The formation of a German Catholic League (1609)
  C. Conflict in Bohemia
        1.   The defenestration that started a war (1618)
        2.   Protestant leaders establish a provisional government
        3.   Outside powers intervene: the conflict spreads
        4.   Count Tilly: Catholic military leader
        5.   The Battle of the White Mountain (1620): a Catholic victory
  D. The Danish period
        1.   The ambitions of Christian IV, Protestant king of the Danes
        2.   Invasion of northern Germany (1625)
        3.   Albert Wallenstein: the leading Catholic general
        4.   The Treaty of Lübeck (1629): Danish retreat

    5.   Emperor Ferdinand II moves fiercely against Protestants
    6.   The Edict of Restitution (1629)
E. The Swedish interlude
    1.   Gustavus Adolphus, Lutheran king of Sweden, enters the fray
    2.   Subduing Catholic Poland and Pomerania
    3.   Ferdinand dismisses Wallenstein
    4.   The Catholic defeat at Breitenfeld (1631)
    5.   The Swedes lose their leader at the Battle of Lützen (1632)
    6.   Wallenstein murdered (1634)
F. The nature of the war
    1.   A vicious orgy of violence
    2.   Religious fanaticism
    3.   Ragtag bands of mercenaries marauding endlessly
G. Dynastic factors
    1.   Two major rivals: France versus Habsburg Austria
    2.   Failure of peace overtures
H. The Treaty of Westphalia (1648)
    1.   Two hundred heads of state participate
    2.   Territorial adjustments that lasted until the French Revolution
    3.   Strong autonomous traditions of the German states
    4.   Calvinists and Lutherans gain equal rights
    5.   The devastation the war left in its wake

Suggestions for Lecture Topics

For a lecture on the St. Bartholomew's Day Massacre, see the vivid details
and background given in Robert M. Kingdon, *Myths about the St.
Bartholomew's Day Massacre*.

Henry IV makes a fascinating figure for a more in-depth biographical
lecture. See David Buisseret, *Henry IV.*

For a lecture on the role played by Richelieu in France see Joseph
Bergin, *Cardinal Richelieu.*

The Thirty Years' War provides an opportunity for a gripping lecture on
religion, violence, and international intrigue, above and beyond the shifting
military fortunes of this protracted conflict. See Geoffrey Parker, *The Thirty
Years' War.*

For biographical studies of some of the major figures, see Golo Mann,
Wallenstein and Michael Roberts, *Gustavus Adolphus.*

Multiple-Choice Questions

1. Which of the following nations did NOT fight in the Thirty Years' War?
   a. Sweden
   b. Denmark
   c. Norway
   d. France
   e. Spain

Answer: c

2. The Concordat of Bologna
   a. reduced the authority of the Catholic Church in France.
   b. increased the authority of the Catholic Church in France.
   c. established peace between French Catholics and Protestants.
   d. separated the Italian state of Bologna from papal rule.
   e. both a and d

Answer: a

3. The Treaty of Cateau-Cambrésis involved which of the following nations?
   a. France and Hungary
   b. France, Spain, and Denmark
   c. France, England, and Sweden
   d. France and Spain
   e. France and Austria

Answer: d

4. Henry of Navarre (Henry IV) came from which noble family?
   a. the house of Navarre
   b. the Bourbon family
   c. the Guise family
   d. the Montmorency family
   e. the Cateau-Cambrésis family

Answer: b

5. Henry IV was
   a. Catholic.
   b. Calvinist.
   c. Lutheran.
   d. Jewish.
   e. Catholic and Calvinist at different times in his life.

Answer: e

6. The Edict of Nantes established
   a.   equal taxation for clergy and nobility.
   b.   the right of Jews to live in France.
   c.   moderate religious toleration for Huguenots.
   d.   Catholicism as the official religion of France.
   e.   both c and d

Answer: e

7. Henry IV was assassinated by
   a.   his wife.
   b.   his son.
   c.   agents of Richelieu.
   d.   a monk.
   e.   agents of the king of Spain.

Answer: d

8. Which of the following was NOT a major participant in the Thirty
   Years' War?
   a.   Wallenstein
   b.   Tilly
   c.   Gustavus Adolphus
   d.   Christian IV
   e.   Henry IV

Answer: e

9. The Thirty Years' War started and ended in which years?
   a.   1618 and 1648
   b.   1598 and 1628
   c.   1604 and 1634
   d.   1648 and 1678
   e.   none of the above

Answer: a

10. Gustavus Adolphus died
    a.   of old age.
    b.   at the Battle of Breitenfeld.
    c.   at the Battle of Lützen.
    d.   at the Battle of the White Mountain.
    e.   in the Defenestration of Prague.

Answer: c

Short-Answer Questions

1. What was the relation between dynastic concerns and religious issues in the French civil strife of the sixteenth century?
2. What was the relation between dynastic concerns and religious issues in the Thirty Years' War?
3. Would it be reasonable to describe Henry IV as a pragmatist? Explain your answer.
4. What were the causes of the Thirty Years' War?
5. Why did the Thirty Years' War last as long as it did?

True/False Questions

1. In the Defenestration of Prague, two Catholic emissaries were hurled to their deaths from a window.

Answer: F

2. Cardinal Richelieu was a member of the powerful Guise family.

Answer: F

3. Under King Louis XIII, the French state was further centralized.

Answer: T

4. In the Thirty Years' War, Lutherans and Calvinists fought each other as bitterly as they fought against Catholics.

Answer: F

5. The duke of Sully was responsible for the assassination of Henry IV.

Answer: F

6. The Edict of Restitution brought a lasting religious peace to the German states.

Answer: F

7. The Thirty Years' War began in Bohemia.

Answer: T

8. The Treaty of Westphalia reaffirmed the principle of *Cuius regio, eius religio*.

Answer: T

9. The Thirty Years' War resulted in the strengthening of the Holy Roman Empire.

Answer: F

10. Gustavus Adolphus conquered Poland and Pomerania.

Answer: T

Chronology

Place the following items in correct chronological order.

    5. Formation of the German Catholic League
    9. Wallenstein murdered
    4. Edict of Nantes
    2. St. Bartholomew's Day Massacre
    10. Treaty of Westphalia
    7. Defenestration of Prague
    8. Battle of the White Mountain
    6. Assassination of Henry IV
    1. Concordat of Bologna
    3. Henry IV becomes king

Part Two
Statemaking

Chapter 5
The Rise of the Atlantic Economy: Spain and England

This chapter describes the gradual shift in economic and military power from the Mediterranean to the Atlantic seaboard. It describes the socioeconomic and cultural preconditions for the rise and decline of Spain, and for the steady ascent of England under the Tudor dynasty.

Chapter Outline

I. Economic expansion
   A. Agricultural productivity increasing in the West
      1. A key precondition for population growth
   B. Rural, or "cottage," industry
   C. New trading patterns
      1. Innovative banking and financial services
      2. Merchant capitalists
      3. Spanish gold and silver from the Americas
      4. Joint-stock companies
      5. Overseas expansion of markets
   D. Inflation, or the "price revolution"
   E. Economic depression of the early 1600s

II. The rise of Spain
   A. The linking of Castile and Aragon
      1. Marriage of Ferdinand and Isabella (1469)
      2. Devotion to the Catholic Church
      3. Struggles with the nobility
      4. Independent traditions within Catalonia and Valencia
   B. The role of American precious metals
   C. The wool trade

III. Spanish expansion
   A. Interdynastic marriages
   B. The Austrian and Spanish Habsburgs
   C. Philip II's empire: the peak of Spanish power
      1. A vast royal bureaucracy
      2. The Escorial and the rituals of monarchy
      3. Combating the Turks
      4. The Battle of Lepanto (1571)

IV. The rise of England
   A. The Tudor dynasty founded (1485)
      1. Henry VII strengthens royal authority
      2. Justices of the peace
   B. Henry VIII's desire for empire
   C. Mary Tudor and religious conflict
   D. The subjugation of Ireland and Scotland

V. The Elizabethan age
   A. Religious divisions
      1. The Thirty-Nine Articles (1563)
      2. Puritanism, the English version of Calvinism
      3. The Scottish Reformation
      4. The execution of the Catholic Mary Stuart
   B. A war deemed inevitable: the Spanish-English conflict
      1. The defeat of the Spanish Armada (1588)
   C. Royal patronage
   D. Elizabeth's fiscal frugality
   E. Centralization of the monarchy
   F. A rapidly growing economy
      1. Rising population
      2. Agricultural boom
      3. Enclosures
      4. Plentiful natural resources
      5. Textile manufacturing
   G. Increasing interests in foreign empire
      1. London becomes Europe's leading capital of trade
      2. The East India Company (1599)
      3. The Virginia settlements (1584–1587)

VI. English society in the Tudor period
   A. A strict hierarchy

      1. Perquisites of the nobility
      2. The yeomanry
      3. Guilds
      4. Smallholders
      5. The poor
   B. An iron fist for social order
      1. Economic hardship
      2. Crime
      3. Elizabethan visions of natural hierarchy
      4. The Poor Laws of 1598 and 1601
   C. Elizabethan theater
      1. Shakespeare

VII. The decline of Spain
   A. The Dutch revolt
      1. Resisting the Inquisition
      2. The sanguinary Duke of Alba
   B. Economic decline
      1. Harvest failures and disease
      2. Inflation
      3. New taxes, inefficiently collected
      4. The expulsion of the Moriscos (1609) backfires
      5. Foreign competition
      6. The costs of empire
      7. A parasitic elite
      8. Cervantes' *Don Quixote*: a parable of national decline
   C. Philip IV's vain attempt at revitalization
      1. The duke of Olivares
      2. The burdens of a global empire
   D. The shift of economic primacy to northwestern Europe

Suggestions for Lecture Topics

For a magisterial description of Mediterranean society, centered around the
Spain of Philip II, see Fernand Braudel's *Annaliste* work, *The Mediterranean*.

    A lecture on Elizabethan England would go well together with the as-
signment of a Shakespeare play such as *The Merry Wives of Windsor* or a sim-
ilar play set in contemporary England.

    Students will enjoy hearing a more detailed account of the sinking of
the Spanish Armada. See Garrett Mattingly, *The Armada*.

For a lecture on the Dutch rebellion against Spanish domination, see Geoffrey Parker, *The Dutch Revolt*.

For background information on the economic transformation occurring during these years, see Carlo Cipolla, *Before the Industrial Revolution*.

Multiple-Choice Questions

1. Examples of the innovative financial and banking services introduced in the fifteenth and sixteenth centuries are
   a. joint-stock companies.
   b. double-entry bookkeeping.
   c. bills of exchange.
   d. all of the above
   e. b and c only

Answer: d

2. The two principal regions of Spain linked by the marriage of Ferdinand and Isabella were
   a. Andorra and Andalusia.
   b. Castile and Granada.
   c. Castile and Aragon.
   d. Valencia and Portugal.
   e. Catalonia and Toledo.

Answer: c

3. The climatic conditions in Spain were favorable to which of the following agricultural products?
   a. wool and wine
   b. cotton and lettuce
   c. pigs and beef
   d. cotton and rice
   e. none of the above

Answer: a

4. The two Spanish regions with the most strongly entrenched traditions of local self-rule and independence were
   a. Catalonia and Granada.
   b. Toledo and Aragon.
   c. Valencia and Portugal.

    d.   Castile and Madrid.
    e.   Catalonia and Valencia.

Answer: e

5. The Habsburg dynasty had two branches, the
    a.   Austrian and Dutch.
    b.   Spanish and Italian.
    c.   Austrian and Spanish.
    d.   German and Spanish.
    e.   French and Spanish.

Answer: c

6. The Escorial was
    a.   a cruel form of punishment.
    b.   a pithy Spanish insult.
    c.   a famous ship.
    d.   a palace.
    e.   a secret society.

Answer: d

7. Which of the following monarchs presided over the apogee of Spanish power?
    a.   Philip II
    b.   Alfonso XIII
    c.   Ferdinand the Magnificent
    d.   Pedro the Bold
    e.   Isabella of Aragon

Answer: a

8. England's Queen Elizabeth I
    a.   left no heirs.
    b.   was a devout Catholic.
    c.   married twice, but had both her husbands killed.
    d.   encouraged the centralization of the monarchy.
    e.   both a and d

Answer: e

9. Mary Tudor was
    a.   the daughter of Henry VIII.
    b.   the sister of Henry VIII.

    c.   the mother of Elizabeth I.
    d.   the daughter of Elizabeth I.
    e.   none of the above

Answer: a

10. English society in the Tudor period was
    a.   rigorously egalitarian.
    b.   strictly hierarchical.
    c.   fraught with religious divisions.
    d.   both b and c
    e.   both a and c

Answer: d

Short-Answer Questions

1. What were some of the principal reasons for the shift of economic and military power to the Atlantic seaboard during the fifteenth and sixteenth centuries?
2. Describe the religious tensions between Protestants and Catholics in Tudor England. What kinds of conflicts did this religious division produce?
3. What were some of the factors that rendered Elizabeth I a great monarch?
4. What was the status of the poor in Elizabethan England? Describe the relations among the various social classes, and the worldview that underpinned these social relations.
5. What were the principal causes for the decline of Spain as a great power, in contrast to the continuing ascent of England?

True/False Questions

1. The duke of Alba was conciliatory toward the Dutch.

Answer: F

2. Mary Stuart was executed because she was a Catholic.

Answer: T

3. Spanish gold and silver from the Americas strengthened the Spanish economy in the short run but weakened it in the long run by causing inflation.

Answer: T

4. Elizabeth I did away with royal patronage, which she considered corrupt.

Answer: F

5. An English yeoman was the equivalent of a serf.

Answer: F

6. Cervantes' *Don Quixote* was a literary description of Spain's national decline.

Answer: T

7. The duke of Olivares aspired to become Spain's new king.

Answer: F

8. During the Elizabethan period, London became Europe's third-largest city.

Answer: F

9. The agents of the Spanish Inquisition tortured people in the name of Christian faith.

Answer: T

10. Ireland and Scotland succesfully resisted subjection by the English during the Tudor period.

Answer: F

Chronology

Place the following items in correct chronological order.
   7. Duke of Alba sent to crush rebellious Dutch
   2. Tudor dynasty founded
   4. The Thirty-Nine Articles
   6. Battle of Lepanto
   1. Marriage of Ferdinand and Isabella of Spain
   9. Defeat of the Spanish Armada
   8. Virginia settlements in the New World
   10. Expulsion of the Moriscos from Spain
   3. Elizabeth I becomes queen
   5. William Shakespeare born

Chapter 6
England and the Dutch Republic in the Seventeenth Century

This chapter narrates the English Civil War and "Glorious Revolution," setting forth the underlying causes for this protracted constitutional struggle, and describing the course of the conflict in detail. The chapter then turns to the Netherlands, describing the golden age that this nation enjoyed in the wake of its independence from Spain.

Chapter Outline

I. Absolutism versus constitutionalism in England and the Netherlands
   A. Religious conflict
   B. Civil liberties in England

II. Background to the English Civil War
   A. The accession of James I (1603)
      1. The union with Scotland
   B. Inefficient means of taxation
      1. Sale of offices and titles
   C. Parliament increasingly asserts its prerogatives
      1. Taxation
      2. Foreign policy
      3. Accountability of ministers
   D. The accession of Charles I (1625)
   E. Religious divisions
      1. The Puritans' challenge
      2. Arminianism: predestination vs. free will
      3. Fears of a "popish plot" to restore Catholicism
   F. Charles I clashes with Parliament
      1. The Petition of Right
      2. Presbyterian rebellion in Scotland

       3.   The dissolution of Parliament (1640)

III. The first phase of the English Civil War
    A. A constitutional deadlock: how to interpret Magna Carta
    B. Fears of a pro-Catholic king
       1.   The Irish rebellion of 1641
    C. Open conflict breaks out: Roundheads vs. Cavaliers
    D. Patterns of allegiance to Parliament and king
       1.   Parliament's alliance with the Scots
       2.   Oliver Cromwell's victory at Marston Moor (1644)
       3.   The "New Model Army"
    E. Divisions with Parliament
       1.   "Presbyterian" moderates
       2.   Independents (militant Puritans)
    F. The royalists defeated (1645)

IV. The second phase of the English Civil War
    A. Social unrest and radical religious groups
       1.   Levellers
       2.   Diggers
       3.   Ranters
    B. The "Rump Parliament" (1648-1653)
       1.   Charging the king with high treason
       2.   The execution of Charles I (1649)
       3.   Abolition of the monarchy: the Commonwealth of England
       4.   International opprobrium
       5.   Cromwell subdues Ireland (1649) and Scotland (1651)
    C. Cromwell's dictatorship
       1.   High-handedness and arbitrary taxation
       2.   Cromwell succeeded by his son Richard (1658)
    D. The monarchy restored
       1.   The accession of Charles II (1660–1661)
       2.   Peace brings renewed economic growth

V. The Glorious Revolution
    A. Renewed religious tensions
       1.   The Test Act (1673)
    B. Tories (royal supremacy) vs. Whigs (parliamentary supremacy)
    C. The *Habeas Corpus* Act (1679)
    D. The accession of the Catholic James II (1685)
    E. James II deposed (1688)

   1. Diplomatic isolation
   2. William of Orange organizes an invasion force
   3. James II goes into exile
  F. The Bill of Rights (1689)
   1. Rights of Parliament
   2. Rights of property
   3. Rule of law
   4. John Locke's philosophy in support of the Revolution
   5. The political power of the gentry

VI. The golden age of the Dutch Republic
  A. The federalist legacy of the Union of Utrecht (1579)
   1. The Estates General
   2. An oligarchical system
   3. Basic rights of citizens
  B. A rapidly growing economy
   1. The Amsterdam Public Bank
   2. Reclaiming territory from the sea
   3. Population growth
   4. A vigorous, competitive merchant trade
   5. The Dutch East India Company (1602)
  C. Religious tolerance
   1. A thriving Jewish community
  D. Prosperity unparalleled
  E. Relative freedom of cultural life
   1. Patronage for the arts
   2. The depiction of everyday life
   3. Rembrandt

VII. The decline of Dutch power
  A. Wars against England
  B. The implacable hostility of France
  C. An increasingly rigid social hierarchy

Suggestions for Lecture Topics

For a recent overview of the scholarly debates over the causes of the English Civil War, see R. C. Richardson, *The Debate on the English Civil War Revisited.* Though too complex for most undergraduates, the book provides a useful historiographical background that will help with writing lectures.

The film *Winstanley* provides a vivid evocation of the English Civil War period, and is likely to stimulate students to engage in a lively discussion of both religious and constitutional issues. The film narrates the life of Gerard Winstanley and his group of Diggers as they pursue their utopian goals amid the turmoil of Cromwell's England.

For a recent biography of Oliver Cromwell that provides plenty of good material for lectures, see Barry Coward, *Oliver Cromwell*. An older, but still excellent biography is Christopher Hill, *God's Englishman*.

The background to the proclamation of the Bill of Rights is the subject of Lois Schwoerer, *The Declaration of Rights, 1689*.

A much-praised work on the Dutch "golden age" is Simon Schama, *The Embarassment of Riches*.

For an in-depth look at the Dutch economy detailing the reasons for this small country's remarkable prosperity, see Jan De Vries, *The Dutch Rural Economy in the Golden Age*.

Multiple-Choice Questions

1. Which English monarch was executed in 1649?
   a. James I
   b. James II
   c. Charles I
   d. Charles II
   e. William of Orange

Answer: c

2. Which of the following was NOT a key issue in the English Civil War?
   a. fear of Catholic influence within the monarchy
   b. charges of absolutist behavior on the part of the king
   c. Parliament's desire for sharing power with the king
   d. anger at the foreign wars that had depleted the nation's treasury
   e. the rise to power of ambitious Puritan leaders

Answer: d

3. The Roundheads were:
   a. on the side of Parliament.
   b. on the side of the king.
   c. on the side of the Anglican church against the Puritans.
   d. a radical religious group whose members cut their hair to show their piety.

   e.   none of the above

Answer: a

4. The "Rump Parliament" was so named because it
   a.   was led by a man named Josiah Rumpe.
   b.   was disbanded forcibly by Charles II.
   c.   was prevented from meeting with all its members present.
   d.   was guilty of charging the king with high treason.
   e.   none of the above

Answer: c

5. Which of the following religious groups was the most radical?
   a.   the Levellers
   b.   the Diggers
   c.   the Ranters
   d.   the Lollards
   e.   the Cavaliers

Answer: c

6. The Test Act of 1673 was designed to
   a.   establish standards in English schools.
   b.   establish religious standards for holding government office.
   c.   establish whether one was a true Protestant.
   d.   establish whether one was a true Catholic.
   e.   establish that no Catholic could convert to Protestantism and then become Catholic again.

Answer: b

7. The structure of the government of the Dutch Republic was
   a.   federalist.
   b.   oligarchical.
   c.   monarchical.
   d.   centralized.
   e.   pluralistic.

Answer: a

8. The flourishing Dutch economy was based principally on
   a.   textiles.
   b.   flowers and agricultural products.
   c.   spices.

    d.   banking and trade.

    e.   none of the above

Answer: d

9. Jews in Holland
   a. were persecuted more fiercely than in other parts of Europe.
   b. enjoyed relative toleration.
   c. converted by the thousands to Catholicism.
   d. converted by the thousands to Protestantism.
   e. were persecuted by Catholics but tolerated by Protestants.

Answer: b

10. Oliver Cromwell was
   a. born Catholic but converted to Protestantism.
   b. born Protestant but converted to Catholicism.
   c. the first Jew to become prominent in English public affairs.
   d. a devout Puritan.
   e. none of the above

Answer: d

Short-Answer Questions

1. What were the principal reasons for many English citizens' fears of "popish plots" and of a Catholic restoration?
2. What was at stake in the conflict between Charles I and Parliament? Explain in detail.
3. Why is the Glorious Revolution regarded as a major milestone in English history?
4. Why was the century after 1648 described as the golden age of the Netherlands?
5. What factors led to the decline in Dutch power as the seventeenth century drew to a close?

True/False Questions

1. Oliver Cromwell's forces were defeated at the battle of Marston Moor, but managed to rally the next year and stage a comeback.

Answer: F

2. Arminianism is a religious doctrine that challenges the notion of pre-destination.

Answer: T

3. The "New Model Army" fought valiantly for Charles I.

Answer: F

4. The British monarchy was abolished in 1649.

Answer: T

5. The British monarchy was restored in 1688.

Answer: F

6. Charles II was a relatively popular king.

Answer: T

7. The *Habeas Corpus* Act was strongly promoted by King James II.

Answer: F

8. The Amsterdam Public Bank was housed in the Amsterdam town hall.

Answer: T

9. The Dutch painter Rembrandt painted more than eighty self-portraits.

Answer: T

10. Despite its name, the Dutch East India Company traded more with Italy than with the East Indies.

Answer: F

Chronology

Place the following items in correct chronological order.
     8. Test Act
     7. Accession of Charles II
     4. Cromwell's victory at Marston Moor
     3. Accession of Charles I
     5. Dutch gain independence from Spain

6. Beheading of Charles I
10. Glorious Revolution
2. Accession of James I
9. *Habeas Corpus* Act
1. Creation of Dutch East India Company

Chapter 7
The Age of Absolutism, 1650–1720

This chapter describes the theories underpinning absolutist monarchy, the processes through which such monarchies were consolidated, and the lasting changes that these monarchies wrought within the European state system.

Chapter Outline

I.   The spread of absolutism

II. Theories of absolutism
    A. Jean Bodin
    B. Thomas Hobbes
    C. Jacques Bossuet
    D. Distinction between absolute power and arbitrary power
       1. Reason
       2. Tradition
       3. Consultation with constituted bodies

III. Characterizing absolute rule
    A. Geographical variations
    B. Relations between the monarch and nobility
       1. A delicate balance
       2. Loyalty in exchange for privileges
    C. The accentuation of despotism in Eastern Europe
    D. Growth of state structures
       1. Taxation
    E. Expansion of standing armies
       1. New reasons for conflict: royal ambitions
       2. Transportation networks
       3. Credit
       4. A huge drain on the budget

    F.   Absolutism and religion
1. Alliance with established churches
2. Limiting ecclesiastical autonomy
    a. The Gallican Church as a case in point
3. Symbiosis between Russian Orthodox Church and tsarist autocracy
4. The Ottoman Empire
    a. The "holy war"
    b. Toleration of religious diversity
    G. Architecture and art
1. Monumentalism: glorifying the monarch
2. The "Louis XIV" style

IV. French absolutism
    A. The most powerful state in Europe
    B. The Fronde
1. Accession of Louis XIV (1643)
2. Cardinal Mazarin
3. Nobles' rebellion against the king's authority (1648)
4. The prince of Condé arrested (1650)
5. The king's triumph (1652)
    C. Mercantilism
1. The calculations of Colbert
2. Nobles and clergy exempt from taxes in France
3. National self-sufficiency and balance of payments
4. New trading companies founded
    D. Louis XIV's style
1. Expropriation of Vaux-le-Vicomte
2. Royal garrisons
3. Intendants
4. A royal propaganda machine
5. An effective bureaucracy
6. Extensive use of patronage to keep nobility loyal
    a. Sale of offices and the expansion of the nobility
    E. Versailles
1. A staging ground for absolutism
2. Ten thousand nobles in attendance at the palace
3. Molière: entertaining and criticizing
    F. Persecution of religious minorities
1. The Huguenots, or French Protestants

      2. Revocation of the Edict of Nantes (1685)

      3. Jansenists: asceticism and an emphasis on divine grace

      4. Jansenists' enemies: the Jesuits

  G. Limits to the king's absolute rule

      1. Local networks of power

      2. Provincial estates and parlements

      3. "We entreat you but we also command you"

V. The Austrian Habsburgs

  A. The 300 German states of the Holy Roman Empire

      1. No centralized power in foreign policy

  B. Habsburg Austria: largest state of the Holy Roman Empire

      1. Division into two parts, Austrian and Spanish (1556)

  C. Nobles more jealous of their prerogatives in Austria than in France

      1. A monarchy balanced between Western and Eastern Europe

      2. A polyglot structure of territories and nationalities

      3. Hungarian spirit of independence

  D. Struggles with the Ottoman empire

VI. Prussia

  A. All the essential components of absolutist success

  B. The Hohenzollern dynasty

  C. The power of Prussian Junkers (noble landowners)

      1. Serfdom grows in sixteenth century

  D. Frederick William, the "Great Elector"

      1. Building a standing army with noble consent

      2. New territories acquired

      3. Setting a standard for efficient bureaucracy

  E. Frederick William I continues his grandfather's state-building

  F. The primacy of the military in the Prussian identity

VII. The Russian empire

  A. Growth of the Duchy of Muscovy

      1. Ivan IV ("the Terrible")

      2. The "Time of Troubles" (starting in 1584)

      3. The defeat of Stephen Razin's peasant rebellion (1670)

      4. The establishment of serfdom (1649) cements nobles to the tsar

  B. The Swedish empire

      1. Charles XI and Charles XII

      2. Tensions between absolutism and parliamentary rule

  C. The rise of Peter the Great in Russia

1. Administrative and military reforms on the Western model
2. Building up a powerful military machine
3. Turning the nobility into an instrument of state
4. Resistance to Westernizing reforms
5. Expansion at the expense of Swedes, Poles, and Turks
6. St. Petersburg, a "window on the West"

VIII. The balance of power
   A. No single country should be allowed to amass disproportionate power
   B. International law
      1. Grotius
      2. Pufendorf
   C. The dynastic wars of Louis XIV
      1. Shifting alliances
      2. The War of the Spanish Succession
      3. The Treaty of Utrecht (1713)
      4. A case of French overreaching
   D. The modern state

Suggestions for Lecture Topics

A slide show on Versailles provides students with vivid insight into the monumentalism of absolutist monarchy.

An interesting recent book on Louis XIV is Peter Burke, *The Fabrication of Louis XIV*. This material would go well with a lecture on the deliberate creation of an imagery of royalty during this period.

Students are often interested in the German military tradition. A standard work on this subject is Gordon Craig's *The Politics of the Prussian Army, 1640–1945*.

For a lecture on Peter the Great, see Nicholas Riasanovsky, *The Image of Peter the Great in Russian History and Thought*.

For a lecture on mercantilism, see Richard Bonney, *Society and Government in France under Richelieu and Mazarin*.

Multiple-Choice Questions

1. Which of the following was NOT a theorist who supported absolutist monarchy?

    a. Jean Bodin
    b. Thomas Hobbes
    c. Jacques Bossuet
    d. John Locke
    e. none of the above

Answer: d

2. Which of the following was NOT a factor intimately related to the rise of absolutist monarchies in Europe?
    a. the growth of bureaucracies
    b. monumentalism in the arts
    c. the expansion of standing armies
    d. the growth of population
    e. limitations on the power of the nobility

Answer: d

3. Absolutist monarchy found its apogee in
    a. France.
    b. England.
    c. Russia.
    d. Germany.
    e. Spain.

Answer: a

4. The Fronde was
    a. a conspiracy to bring a Huguenot to the throne of France.
    b. a conspiracy of nobles to limit monarchical power.
    c. a plot to kill the king.
    d. a plot hatched by Cardinal Richelieu against the young Louis XIV.
    e. none of the above

Answer: b

5. The man who presided over the French monarchy during the youth of Louis XIV was
    a. Cardinal Richelieu.
    b. the prince of Condé.
    c. Cardinal Mazarin.
    d. René Descartes.
    e. Jean-Baptiste Colbert.

Answer: c

6. The noble dynasty of Prussia was
   a.   the Habsburgs.
   b.   the Mayerlings.
   c.   the Wilhelms.
   d.   the Junkers.
   e.   the Hohenzollerns.

Answer: e

7. The Huguenots were
   a.   French Protestants.
   b.   followers of a man named Johan Hugh.
   c.   Dutch missionaries.
   d.   a Swedish religious order.
   e.   French atheists.

Answer: a

8. Peter the Great expanded the Duchy of Muscovy primarily at the expense of which of the following peoples?
   a.   Swedes, Turks, and Chinese
   b.   Germans and Poles
   c.   Mongols and Turks
   d.   Swedes and Persians
   e.   Swedes, Turks, and Poles

Answer: e

9. The Treaty of Utrecht concluded which of the following wars?
   a.   the Dutch-English War
   b.   the Thirty Years' War
   c.   the War of the Spanish Succession
   d.   the Austro-Prussian War
   e.   the War of Jenkins' Ear

Answer: c

10. Absolutist rulers tended to:
    a.   forge alliances with established churches.
    b.   limit ecclesiastical autonomy.
    c.   try to create their own national churches.
    d.   all of the above
    e.   only a and b

Answer: e

Short-Answer Questions

1. On what grounds did philosophers like Bodin, Hobbes, and Bossuet defend the practice of absolutism?
2. Describe the convergence of interests between monarchs and nobles that made absolutism possible. In what ways did absolutism provide both the nobility and the monarch with mutual benefits?
3. What was the motivation for the Fronde?
4. Describe the process by which absolutist monarchy was established by the Hohenzollerns of Prussia. What are the major "ingredients" of absolutist rule?
5. What is meant by the term "balance of power," and how is this concept reflected in the statecraft of the seventeenth century in Europe?

True/False Questions

1. Ivan IV of Russia was a cruel king, nicknamed "the Terrible."

Answer: T

2. The Jansenists were an English religious sect that believed there was no afterlife after death.

Answer: F

3. The Junkers were Prussian landowning nobles.

Answer: T

4. The ability to raise taxes was an important factor in the building of absolutist monarchies.

Answer: T

5. Absolutism was in practice the same as arbitrary rule, in the sense that the monarch was free to do whatever he wanted to his or her subjects.

Answer: F

6. Frederick William I of Prussia was a weak ruler who dissipated the gains made by his grandfather.

Answer: F

7. Serfdom was finally abolished in Russia in 1649.

Answer: F

8. Hugo Grotius was a merchant who became Europe's first millionaire.

Answer: F

9. Louis XIV reinstated religious persecution in France after 1685.

Answer: T

10. Peter the Great sought to exert a "Westernizing" influence on Russia.

Answer: T

Chronology

Place the following items in correct chronological order.
4. Accession to throne of Louis XIV
8. Defeat of Stephen Razin's peasant rebellion
2. "Time of Troubles" begins in Russia
5. Beginning of the Fronde
10. Treaty of Utrecht
6. Legal establishment of serfdom in Russia
1. Division of Habsburg domains into Austrian and Spanish parts
9. Revocation of the Edict of Nantes by Louis XIV
3. Proclamation of the Edict of Nantes by Henry IV
7. Publication of Hobbes' *Leviathan*

Part Three
New Cultural and Political Horizons

Chapter 8
The New Philosophy of Science

This chapter describes the cumulative transformation of cosmology, and of the human understanding of nature, that culminated in Europe with the rise of new scientific institutions in the sixteenth century.

Chapter Outline

I. Changing views of the universe
    A. The long reach of Aristotle
        1. A geocentric, hierarchical order
        2. Rest as a nobler state than motion
        3. Ptolemy's astronomy
        4. The influence of Church doctrine
        5. Dante's concentric cosmology
    B. The impact of the Renaissance
    C. The Copernican challenge
        1. Publication of his observations (1543)
        2. The heliocentric vision
    D. New understanding of human anatomy
        1. Galen and the four bodily humors
        2. Vesalius (1514–1564) begins systematic study and dissection
        3. Harvey and the circulation of blood
    E. Tycho Brahe and Johannes Kepler: a new standard in astronomy
        1. Elliptical orbits for the planets
        2. Postulating the force of gravity
    F. Bacon's scientific method
        1. The primacy of observation and experimentation
    G. Galileo: science on trial
        1. The importance of the University of Padua
        2. The impact of the telescope
        3. A theory of inertia: standing Aristotle on his head

     4. Dragged before the Inquisition (1633)

     5. Forced recantation

II. Descartes versus Newton

    A. Cartesian deductive reasoning: from abstract premises to conclusion

    B. Publication of *Discourse on Method* (1637)

       1. *Cogito, ergo sum*: the starting point

       2. Mind and matter

       3. God as the divine clockmaker who creates, then becomes absent

    C. Mathematics as an epistemological model

    D. Newton: a synthesis of Galileo's empiricism and Cartesian logic

       1. Publication of the *Principia* (1687)

       2. A remarkable range of pioneering achievements

    E. Success and acclaim within his own lifetime

    F. Newton's continued activity and self-perception as a theologian

    G. The Cartesians' ally: Spinoza

    H. Leibniz's vision of an infinite universe

III. The culture of science

    A. Scientific method spreads

    B. Formation of the Royal Society (1662)

       1. Halley, Locke, and Wren as members

    C. Margaret Cavendish, a woman scientist working in isolation

    D. Founding of the French Royal Academy of Science (1666)

       1. Enjoying royal patronage

       2. Colbert: putting science to practical use

    E. From Western to Eastern Europe: diminishing scientific activity

       1. Opposition from the Russian Orthodox Church

    F. Emerging applications in technology

       1. Science in the service of the state

    G. Science and religion

       1. The implacable hostility of Catholic and Orthodox clerics

       2. Protestantism: a theology more open to scientific inquiry

       3. The Netherlands as a haven for persecuted scientists

       4. The English Civil War and scientific freedom

       5. State censorship in France

    H. Long-term ramifications

       1. From the natural world to the social world

Suggestions for Lecture Topics

For a lecture on the "big picture" of scientific innovation and change, see Thomas Kuhn, *The Structure of Scientific Revolutions*.

With this topic, concrete examples and a slide show would probably help to make students understand more clearly the tentative, halting, and often error-ridden process through which "scientific method" emerged.

For a lecture designed for advanced undergraduates, a sophisticated approach to discussing the emergence of science is contained in Steven Shapin, *A Social History of Truth*, in Thomas Laqueur, *Making Sex*, and in Bruno Latour, *We Have Never Been Modern*. Though these books themselves make rather challenging reading for undergraduates, they contain many ideas that could lead to a provocative and interesting lecture.

For a lecture on the role of women in science, see Londa Schiebinger, *The Mind Has No Sex?*

For a lecture on Galileo, see Mario Biagioli, *Galileo, the Courtier*.

For a lecture on Newton, see Richard Westfall, *Life of Isaac Newton*.

Multiple-Choice Questions

1. Which of the following was NOT one of the bodily humors postulated by Galen?
   a. blood
   b. saliva
   c. phlegm
   d. yellow bile
   e. black bile

Answer: b

2. Cartesians were
   a. the followers of the Cartan heresy.
   b. English believers in Magna Carta.
   c. the followers of Descartes.
   d. a French monastic group engaged in scientific inquiry.
   e. none of the above

Answer: c

3. *Cogito, ergo sum* means:
   a. Cognition comes before all.

   b.   To reflect is the highest human aim.
   c.   No action is without a corresponding reaction.
   d.   God is great.
   e.   I think, therefore I am.

Answer: e

4. Which of the following ancient Greek philosophers possessed the most long-lasting influence on the later development of science?
    a.   Aristotle
    b.   Plato
    c.   Heraclitus
    d.   Ptolemy
    e.   Galen

Answer: a

5. Which of the following was one of Europe's first women scientists?
    a.   Mary Shelley
    b.   Margaret Cavendish
    c.   Thérèse Levasseur
    d.   Madame de Staël
    e.   Hildegard von Bingen

Answer: b

6. After being put on trial by the Inquisition, Galileo
    a.   defiantly continued to proclaim the truth of his findings.
    b.   was burned at the stake as a heretic.
    c.   recanted his findings.
    d.   escaped and went to Holland.
    e.   none of the above

Answer: c

7. Which of the following religious currents was most hostile to science?
    a.   Jansenism
    b.   Catholicism
    c.   Islam
    d.   Protestantism
    e.   All of these were equally hostile to science.

Answer: b

8. Colbert believed that

   a.   French science was natually superior to English science.
   b.   science and religion could be reconciled.
   c.   science and religion could not be reconciled.
   d.   science should be made an instrument of a mercantilist state policy.
   e.   none of the above

Answer: d

  9. Tycho Brahe was
   a.   a physician.
   b.   a mathematician.
   c.   a grinder of optical lenses.
   d.   an astronomer.
   e.   all of the above

Answer: d

 10. For Descartes, the two primary aspects of the universe were
   a.   mind and matter.
   b.   fire and spirit.
   c.   earth and heaven.
   d.   God and creation.
   e.   none of the above

Answer: a

Short-Answer Questions

  1. Briefly describe the main elements of Aristotle's view of the cosmos.
      Why was the influence of this vision so far-reaching? Explain.
  2. Why was there so much resistance to the heliocentric vision of the
      world put forth by Copernicus?
  3. What was new about the various forms of scientific inquiry that began
      to make their appearance in Europe after the Renaissance, and that
      culminated in the seventeenth and eighteenth centuries?
  4. What was at stake in the two opposed positions embodied by Descartes
      and Newton? What is the distinction between inductive and deductive
      reasoning?
  5. Why were many of the established churches of Europe so hostile to the
      new scientific worldview, despite the fact that most scientists continued
      to remain deeply pious individuals?

True/False Questions

1. Aristotle considered rest a nobler state than motion.

Answer: T

2. Ptolemy's conception of the universe was geocentric.

Answer: T

3. Margaret Cavendish became the first woman member of the English Royal Society.

Answer: F

4. The story about Isaac Newton and the falling apple is actually a false one.

Answer: F

5. The sixteenth century should be seen primarily as an era of conceptual innovation rather than technological innovation.

Answer: T

6. As one went from Western Europe toward Eastern Europe, one would find the state of scientific inquiry less and less advanced.

Answer: T

7. Spinoza was an ally of the Cartesians.

Answer: T

8. On balance, the English Civil War probably exerted a favorable impact on that nation's scientific advance.

Answer: T

9. The University of Padua was a major center for theology, and hence became famous for its persecution of scientists.

Answer: F

10. Sir Francis Bacon was charged and convicted of accepting bribes.

Answer: T

Chronology

Place the following items in correct chronological order.

   9. Founding of the French Royal Academy of Science

   4. Publication of Copernicus' astronomical theory

   1. Aristotle born

 10. Publication of Newton's *Principia*

   2. Ptolemy born

   7. Publication of Descartes' *Discourse on Method*

   8. Formation of the English Royal Society

   6. Galileo placed on trial

   3. Leonardo da Vinci died

   5. Publication of Vesalius' *On the Fabric of the Human Body*

Chapter 9
Eighteenth–Century Economic and Social Change

This chapter details the transformation of the European socioeconomic system as a traditional "society of orders" began to be challenged by an emerging "society of mobility." It focuses on the conditions of life for the various social classes, and on the economic forces that helped shape and modify these conditions.

Chapter Outline

I.   The social order
    A.   A hierarchy of estates or orders
    B.   Nobility
        1.   Between 1 and 15 percent of the population
        2.   Land ownership
        3.   Seigneurial rights
        4.   Exemption from taxes
        5.   Trial by nobles
        6.   Expectations of deference
    C.   Significant gradations of wealth and status within the nobility
        1.   Impoverished nobles
    D.   The British landed elite
        1.   Primogeniture
        2.   Setting an example for the lower orders
        3.   Schooling
    E.   Clergy: reflecting the broader social hierarchy
        1.   Lower clergy vs. bishops
    F.   The "middling sort"
        1.   A broad range of wealth and influence
        2.   The legal profession
    G.   Peasants: the vast majority

    1. Scorned by the upper classes
    2. Village life
    3. Regional differences throughout Europe
    4. Debt
    5. Serfdom dying out in Western Europe, still prevalent in Eastern Europe
    6. Draconian powers of nobility over peasantry
    7. Pugachev's Rebellion (1773–1774): every nobleman's nightmare

II. Signs of the early Industrial Revolution
  A. New agricultural methods
    1. Crop rotation replaces fallow fields
    2. Enclosures: more than one-fourth of England's farmland
    3. Central and Eastern Europe: far more primitive conditions
    4. A broad change in the weather of Europe
    5. Improved animal husbandry
    6. Model farms
  B. Population growth in Europe
    1. From 120 million to 190 million in the eighteenth century
    2. Illness and epidemics still take a toll
    3. Professionalization of armies lowers civilian war casualties
    4. Malthusian fears, published in 1798
  C. Manufacturing
    1. The survival of guilds
    2. The putting-out system: domestic industry in rural areas
    3. Textiles, women, and children
  D. Technological change
    1. Iron
    2. Inventions in spinning and weaving
    3. Water and steam power
    4. Hargreaves' "spinning jenny"
    5. The emergence of factory production
    6. Disciplining and punishing workers
  E. England's economic advantages
    1. Political and linguistic unity
    2. A wealthy polity
    3. Raw materials from colonies
    4. Early development of banking and trading practices
    5. Good transportation networks: macadamization and canals
    6. Government encouragement of trade

       7.   Adam Smith and laissez-faire
   F. Economies on the continent
       1.   The growth of global trade
       2.   Problems of credit and capital
       3.   France racing to keep up with Britain

III. The emergence of a mobile society
   A. Towns and cities
       1.   Steady urban growth, draining the rural areas
       2.   New manufacturing towns like Liverpool and Manchester
       3.   City life: luxury and entertainments
   B. The mobility of the middle classes
       1.   Purchasing noble titles (common everywhere but in Britain)
       2.   The growth of a large middle class in Britain
       3.   France: the Ségur Law of 1782, restricting military titles
       4.   Barriers breaking down between nobility and middle class
   C. The changing condition of the poor
       1.   Proliferation of paupers
       2.   Criminality
       3.   The abyss of the urban indigents
       4.   The inadequacies of charity

IV. Social control
   A. Protecting property
       1.   Property and the right to vote
       2.   Hunting and poaching
   B. Policing the poor
       1.   Temporary poor relief
       2.   Workhouses
       3.   Executions as public spectacles
       4.   "Deserving" and "undeserving" poor
       5.   Brigandage
   C. Stark social contrasts

Suggestions for Lecture Topics

An excellent account of conditions of life for the poor in eighteenth-century England, from which vivid material might be drawn for a lecture, is E.P. Thompson, *Whigs and Hunters*.

For a lecture on criminality during this period, see Peter Linebaugh, *The*

London Hanged. The book contains vivid descriptions that would be likely to galvanize the attention of undergraduates in a lecture.

For a lecture on the status of the various social orders in France and Russia, see J.H. Shennan, *Liberty and Order in Early Modern Europe.*

For a lecture on the status of women during this period, see Vivien Jones, *Women in the Eighteenth Century.*

For a lecture on the early processes of industrialization, see David Landes, *The Unbound Prometheus.*

Multiple-Choice Questions

1. Which of the following was NOT one of the rights of nobles in many parts of Europe during the eighteenth century?
   a.   exemption from taxes
   b.   the right to kill the leaders of one's peasants if they rebelled
   c.   the right to extract goods in kind from peasants
   d.   the right to trial by one's noble peers
   e.   the right to maim any of one's peasants

Answer: b

2. Pugachev's Rebellion was
   a.   a revolt of peasants in Russia.
   b.   a revolt of nobles against the tsar.
   c.   a tax revolt by the middle class in Moscow.
   d.   the title of a novel by Rimski-Korsakov.
   e.   none of the above

Answer: a

3. During the eighteenth century, enclosures took up what percentage of the common land?
   a.   5 percent
   b.   10 percent
   c.   50 percent
   d.   70 percent
   e.   none of the above

Answer: e

4. The inventor of the "spinning jenny" was a man named:
   a.   Jones.

    b.   Watt.
    c.   Boulton.
    d.   Hargreaves.
    e.   Arkwright.

Answer: d

5. The inventor of the steam engine was a man named:
    a. Hargreaves.
    b. Watt.
    c. Boulton.
    d. Arkwright.
    e. none of the above

Answer: b

6. Which of the following was NOT one of the economic advantages enjoyed by England in its early industrialization?
    a. political and linguistic unity
    b. strict government oversight of most business transactions
    c. sophisticated banking and trading practices
    d. raw materials from its colonies
    e. good transportation networks

Answer: b

7. The French Ségur Law of 1782
    a. prohibited beggars from entering Paris.
    b. prohibited nobles from killing peasants.
    c. stated that some nobles would henceforth have to pay certain taxes.
    d. restricted the qualifications of those appointed to military office.
    e. none of the above

Answer: d

8. The amount of money given in charity in the eighteenth century
    a. was low, but growing rapidly.
    b. was high, but declining rapidly.
    c. was high, but insufficient to meet the needs of the poor.
    d. was high, and barely sufficient to meet the needs of the poor.
    e. was highest in the Catholic parts of Europe.

Answer: c

9. The penalty for poaching on private lands in eighteenth-century England was

a. death.
b. to have both one's hands cut off.
c. to be pilloried.
d. to be paraded about town and publicly humiliated.
e. to have to pay a large fine.

Answer: a

10. In the eighteenth century, the population of Europe grew by what
    amount?
    a. from 50 million to 100 million
    b. from 200 million to 300 million
    c. from 300 million to 400 million
    d. from 400 million to 500 million
    e. none of the above

Answer: e

Short-Answer Questions

1. If one traveled from England eastward across Europe toward Russia in
    the eighteenth century, what kinds of national and regional differences
    might one expect to encounter?
2. What were the rights of the nobility in most parts of Europe during
    this period?
3. What were the principal factors accounting for agricultural innovation
    and improved production during this period?
4. Describe the social mobility open to Europeans during this period.
    What chance did one have of moving from one "order" to another?
    Under what conditions might one hope to be able to do so?
5. Why did England advance toward industrialization before other parts
    of Europe? Describe the principal advantages enjoyed by this nation
    over other nations in building up its economy during this period.

True/False Questions

1. Public executions were attended by throngs of people seeking enter-
    tainment.

Answer: T

2. Canals and rivers provided a considerable portion of England's transportation network during the eighteenth century.

Answer: T

3. A factory worker could be fined, but not beaten, if he or she was late to work.

Answer: F

4. In Spain, approximately 15 percent of the population was part of the nobility.

Answer: T

5. Children under age nine were not allowed to work in factories.

Answer: F

6. Purchasing noble titles was uncommon in England.

Answer: T

7. Population growth occurred mainly in rural areas during the eighteenth century.

Answer: F

8. The professionalization of armies led to lower civilian casualties in Europe's wars during this period.

Answer: T

9. Early steam engines were not used for transportation, but for pumping water out of coal pits.

Answer: T

10. In England, the right to vote was directly linked to property ownership.

Answer: T

Chronology

Place the following items in correct chronological order.
6. Pugachev's Rebellion
10. Malthus publishes his work on population

8. France's Ségur Law passed
1. English Glorious Revolution
9. Catherine the Great legally binds Russian serfs to their lords
4. Major smallpox epidemic strikes Paris
3. Abraham Darby invents a procedure for smelting with coke
5. Hargreaves invents spinning jenny
2. Union of England and Scotland, creating Great Britain
7. Adam Smith publishes *The Wealth of Nations*

Chapter 10
Enlightened Thought and the Republic of Letters

This chapter relates the rise of Enlightenment thought throughout Europe in the eighteenth century. It describes the contributions of major intellectual figures, the spread of their influence, and the practical impact of their ideas.

Chapter Outline

I. The Enlightenment spirit: "Dare to know!"
    A. Three stages
        1. Early 1700s; Scientific Revolution
        2. High Enlightenment; from Montesquieu to Voltaire
        3. Late Enlightenment: freedom and the emotions

II. Enlightened ideas
    A. Intellectual origins
        1. The Scientific Revolution
        2. Reason and experimentation
    B. Locke: subjecting philosophy to the rigors of science
        1. Linking natural laws and social laws
        2. The dignity of the individual and the social contract
        3. New visions of marriage
    C. Buffon's experiments
        1. Questioning the biblical account of creation
    D. The Republic of Ideas
        1. An informal international community of philosophes
    E. Montesquieu
        1. The *Persian Letters* (1721): a universal standard of justice
        2. *Spirit of the Laws* (1748): defense of constitutionalism
    F. Voltaire

        1.   Admiring the English restraints on monarchical power
        2.   Attacking the Church and the parlements
        3.   The Calas Affair: a struggle against intolerance
    G. Diderot
        1.   The *Encyclopedia* (1751): greatest monument of the Enlightenment
        2.   Improving the world through systematic critical knowledge
        3.   Disseminating the *Encyclopedia* far and wide
        4.   Royal censorship
    H. Rousseau
        1.   Idealization of emotion, freedom, instinct, spontaneity
        2.   Civilization as a corrupting influence
        3.   *Émile* (1762): an idealized education
        4.   *The Social Contract* (1762): the notion of "general will"

III. The social dimension of the Enlightenment
    A. The decline of religion
        1.   Mounting dissatisfaction
        2.   Britain as the exception: growing religious practice
        3.   Wesley and the birth of Methodism: all are equal before God
    B. Expansion of the cultural base
        1.   Growing literacy
        2.   The spread of publishing
        3.   Interest in historical works
        4.   Reading circles
    C. Art
        1.   Rococo: a new and secular style of elaborate decoration
        2.   Watteau
        3.   Hogarth
    D. Music
        1.   Court composers and patronage
        2.   Mozart's innovations
    E. The spread of Enlightened ideas
        1.   *Salons* and other institutions for the dissemination of ideas
        2.   Increasing politicization
        3.   Academies: serving public and king
        4.   Masonic lodges: freethinkers opposing Church influence
        5.   Censorship

IV. Enlightened absolutism
    A. Reform of jurisprudence

        1. Beccaria's *On Crimes and Punishment* (1764): progressive reforms

  B. Educational reform

  C. Religious toleration

        1. The plight of Jews

        2. Monarchs seize opportunity to weaken Church authority

        3. Portugal's Pombal: hobbling the Jesuits' power

        4. Protestant states: strong interest in religious toleration

  D. Frederick the Great

        1. A philosopher-king

        2. Courtship and clash with Voltaire

        3. Freedom for royal serfs

        4. Enlightened reforms

        5. A more powerful Prussia: increased efficiency of administration

  E. Rural reforms attempted

        1. Maria Theresa of Austria: limiting seigneurial obligations

        2. Joseph II of Austria abolishes serfdom

        3. Leopold of Tuscany's reforms

        4. Catherine the Great of Russia: Charter of the Nobility (1785)

  F. Enlightened statecraft

V. The late Enlightenment

  A. The deaths of Voltaire and Rousseau (1778) herald a new era

  B. Economic theorists: moving away from mercantilism

  C. Physiocrats: land, not gold, as the basis of wealth

        1. Quesnay: calling for an end to royal controls

  D. Adam Smith: classical liberalism, or *laissez-faire*

  E. German idealism

        1. Kant's *Critique of Pure Reason* (1781)

        2. Interest in national cultures

  F. The emergence of "public opinion"

  G. Banned books and the undermining of authority

VI. The legacy of the Enlightenment

  A. Celebration of reason

  B. Belief in progress

  C. Defense of human dignity

  D. Advances of human freedom

Suggestions for Lecture Topics

For a classic interpretive text on the Enlightenment, see Peter Gay, *The Enlightenment*.

For a lecture on Voltaire, see Haydn Mason, *Voltaire*. On the Calas affair, see David Bien, *The Calas Affair*.

Students tend to have a hard time grasping the elusive concept of Rousseau's "general will" (admittedly a slippery notion). A classic work on Rousseau that sheds light on this issue is Ernst Cassirer, *The Question of Jean-Jacques Rousseau*.

Highly recommended for its anecdotes and rich detail on Enlightenment France is Robert Darnton's collection of essays, *The Great Cat Massacre*. Students will appreciate the mixture of "down to earth" stories and reflective analysis that this collection provides.

For a lecture on Enlightened despotism, see Leonard Krieger, *An Essay on the Theory of Enlightenment and Despotism*.

Multiple-Choice Questions

1. Which of the following was the author of *Spirit of the Laws*?
   a. Beccaria
   b. Rousseau
   c. Voltaire
   d. Locke
   e. none of the above

Answer: e

2. In the *Persian Letters*, Montesquieu
   a. describes the Ottoman Empire.
   b. describes France seen through the eyes of two foreign visitors.
   c. praises the English parliamentary system.
   d. wrote a pornographic account of a harem.
   e. none of the above

Answer: b

3. In the Calas Affair, Voltaire
   a. fought a duel with a man named Calas.
   b. saved a man named Calas from execution.
   c. struggled to exculpate a man named Calas after his execution.

    d.   had an affair with the wife of a man named Calas.

    e.   accepted bribes from the mayor of a city named Calas.

Answer: c

4. The *Encyclopedia* is most commonly associated with
   a. Voltaire.
   b. Rameau.
   c. Rousseau.
   d. Diderot.
   e. Turgot.

Answer: d

5. Rousseau's *Émile* is about
   a. an old woman named Émile.
   b. the education of a young man named François by his teacher, Émile.
   c. Rousseau's wife.
   d. the rights of noblemen to resist monarchical absolutism.
   e. none of the above

Answer: e

6. John Wesley's Methodism was based on the idea that
   a. all are equal before God.
   b. the rich should share with the poor.
   c. the poor had a right to seize what they needed from the rich.
   d. the Anglican Church was too corrupt to be open to reform.
   e. God had created an unchangeable hierarchy of people in society.

Answer: a

7. Rousseau
   a. thought that reason should always predominate over emotion.
   b. thought that emotion was just as important as reason.
   c. thought that civilization resulted in steady human progress.
   d. thought that civilization brought a degeneration of humans.
   e. both b and d

Answer: e

8. Rococo was
   a. an artistic style of austere simplicity.
   b. an artistic style of elaborate decorative complexity.
   c. derived from the French words for "rocks" and "bells"

    d.   both a and c

    e.   both b and c

Answer: b

9. Beccaria's *On Crime and Punishment*
   a.   argued for harsher penalties as a deterrent to crime.
   b.   argued for punishment to be proportionate to the harm done by the crime.
   c.   argued in favor of the death penalty.
   d.   both a and c
   e.   none of the above

Answer: b

10. Which of the following was NOT noted as an enlightened reformer?
    a.   Frederick the Great of Prussia
    b.   Maria Theresa of Austria
    c.   Joseph II of Austria
    d.   Leopold of Tuscany
    e.   Louis XV of France

Answer: e

Short-Answer Questions

1. What basic notions did the Enlightenment philosophes have in common? Describe these notions and their reasoning in advancing them.
2. In what ways did the *Encyclopedia* constitute an embodiment of Diderot's Enlightenment optimism?
3. What notion lies at the heart of the term "social contract"? Explain the difference between the interpretations given by Locke and Rousseau of this term.
4. What sort of practical impact, if any, did the Enlightenment ideas produce in the eighteenth century? Discuss with regard to at least two nations.
5. What sort of factors made the difference between the high Enlightenment and the late Enlightenment? What had changed, in the transition from the one to the other?

True/False Questions

1. The *Spirit of the Laws* was written by the same legal reformer as *On Crimes and Punishment*.

Answer: F

2. The Scientific Revolution played an important role in the origins of the Enlightenment.

Answer: T

3. Mozart died in abject poverty.

Answer: T

4. Frederick the Great was so impressed with Enlightenment ideas that he freed the serfs on the royal domains.

Answer: T

5. Frederick the Great was so impressed with Enlightenment ideas that he invited Voltaire to stay with him in Prussia.

Answer: T

6. Kant's *Critique of Pure Reason* was an impassioned philosophical plea for a balance between reason and emotion, based on the idea that the use of reason by itself resulted in unbalanced human beings.

Answer: F

7. The Enlightenment brought some relief for many targets of religious persecution, including Jews.

Answer: T

8. Physiocrats believed that gold, not land, should be the ultimate measure of wealth.

Answer: F

9. The France of the Enlightenment had severe censorship laws.

Answer: T

10. Pornography was widespread in France during the eighteenth century.

Answer: T

Chronology

Place the following items in correct chronological order.

8. Deaths of Voltaire and Rousseau
1. English Glorious Revolution
3. Publication of Montesquieu's *Spirit of the Laws*
2. Publication of Locke's *Essay Concerning Human Understanding*
6. Calas Affair
4. First volume of *Encyclopedia* published
7. Rousseau exiled from Paris, goes to Geneva
10. French Revolution
9. Catherine the Great's Charter of the Nobility
5. Jesuits expelled from Portugal

Chapter 11
Eighteenth-Century Dynastic Rivalries and Politics

This chapter sets forth the political history of eighteenth-century Europe, paying particularly close attention to the case of Britain. It narrates the international rivalries and conflicts that marked the century, as well as the movements for political reform that sprang up in many parts of Europe.

Chapter Outline

I. Balance within nations and among nations

II. The eighteenth-century state system
    A. Marriage, inheritance, and battle as the tools of aggrandizement
    B. Economic rivalries
    C. Colonial expansion
        1. The British East India Company
        2. Spain's vast holdings
        3. French and British in North America
        4. The War of Jenkins' Ear (1739)
    D. The English Hanoverian dynasty
        1. The Act of Succession (1701): preventing Stuart restoration
        2. The Act of Union (1707) links England and Wales to Scotland
        3. Severe restrictions on Catholic rights
        4. The accession of George I (1714)
        5. The accession of George II (1727)
        6. A Stuart bid to retake the throne (1745) with Scottish support
    E. Prussian-Austrian rivalry
        1. The Pragmatic Sanction and accession of Maria Theresa (1740)
        2. Frederick the Great builds up Prussia as a Great Power

III. Great-Power conflicts
    A. The War of the Austrian Succession (1740–1748)

      1.   Frederick's invasion of Habsburg Silesia
      2.   The polyglot Habsburg empire
      3.   Maria Theresa forges an anti-Prussian alliance
      4.   The inconclusive Treaty of Aix-la-Chapelle (1748)
- B. The Seven Years' War (1756–1763)
      1.   A global conflict, from North America to India
      2.   Nationalist enthusiasms in Britain and France
      3.   The "Diplomatic Revolution" of 1756: France and Austria ally
      4.   Prussia and Britain ally
      5.   Franco-British conflict in India
      6.   Robert Clive defeats the French at Plassey (1757)
      7.   British victories over the French in North America
      8.   The Treaty of Paris (1763)
- C. Warfare in the eighteenth century
      1.   Nobles and war
      2.   Recruits and mercenaries
      3.   Desertion
      4.   The role of technology: bayonets and new firearms
      5.   Training and tactics
      6.   Rules of engagement
      7.   Expansion of the British navy

IV. Politics in Great Britain
- A. The legacy of 1688
- B. The House of Commons (1760s)
      1.   Tories: siding with the authority of the throne
      2.   Whigs: championing the rights of Parliament
- C. Powers of the central government
      1.   Debt servicing
      2.   Financial speculation: the South Sea Bubble (1720)
      3.   Robert Walpole becomes chancellor of the Exchequer (1721)
      4.   Walpole's domination of the House of Commons
      5.   Widespread patronage
      6.   Tripling the size of the British military
      7.   A rapidly expanding Treasury
- D. The House of Commons
      1.   The emerging epicenter of political power
      2.   Landed and commercial interests
      3.   A severely limited franchise
- E. Whigs and Tories

   1. George III's insistence on monarchical independence
   2. The question of ministerial responsibility
   3. "Party": not a formal organization, but a current of opinion
   4. The notion of a parliamentary opposition emerges
   5. Tories unconditionally support royal authority
  F. The rise of nationalism
   1. Promoting British commercial predominance
   2. Fear of Catholic powers
   3. Insular pride and imperial destiny
   4. Relative harmony between landed elites and commercial gentry
   5. Constitutional guarantees maintained
   6. Increasingly professional armed forces

V. Challenges to established authority
  A. British radicals
   1. Demanding electoral reforms
   2. John Wilkes and English liberties
   3. A broadening political culture
  B. American revolutionaries
   1. The burgeoning colonies
   2. The Stamp Act (1765) and Townshend Acts (1767)
   3. The Boston Tea Party (1773)
   4. Intolerable Acts (1774)
   5. Thomas Paine and Common Sense (1776)
   6. The Declaration of Independence (1776): Enlightenment influence
   7. The War of Independence (1776–1783)
   8. French support for the rebels
  C. French monarchy and parlements
   1. Challenges to absolutist rule
   2. Challenges to noble privilege
   3. Jansenist dissidents
   4. The Parlement of Paris champions constitutional liberties
   5. Taxation: the nobility adamantly resists
   6. Growing criticism of Louis XV
   7. Turgot's reforms, pushing economic liberalization, fail
  D. Other movements for reform throughout Europe
   1. Federalists vs. centralizers in the Dutch United Provinces

VI. Declining powers: the Ottoman Empire and Poland
  A. Turkish power recedes from Europe

1. Failing to keep pace with Western technology
2. Incapable rulers
3. The weaknesses of indirect rule
4. Russia profits from the Turkish decline

B. Poland gobbled up by its neighbors: Prussia, Russia, and Austria
1. Nobles dominate monarchy
2. Russian hegemony
3. King Stanislas Poniatowski undertakes reforms
4. The First Partition of Poland (1772)
5. The Second Partition (1793)
6. The Third Partition (1795)
7. Poland vanishes as an independent country

Suggestions for Lecture Topics

An interesting thesis, briefly referred to in the text of this chapter, is put forth by Robert R. Palmer in *The Age of the Democratic Revolution*. Though it has been criticized, Palmer's argument that a common wave of democratic sentiments united both sides of the Atlantic in the second half of the eighteenth century makes provocative material for a lecture.

For a lecture on radical politics in Britain, see the vivid material explored by James Epstein in his *Radical Expression*.

Students will find the story of the South Sea Bubble fascinating. See the relevant chapters in Peter Mathias, *The First Industrial Nation*.

On the Seven Years' War, see John Brewer, *The Sinews of Power*.

For a lecture on Maria Theresa of Austria, see William McGill, *Maria Theresa*.

Multiple-Choice Questions

1. Which of the following aimed at preventing a restoration of the Stuart dynasty to the English monarchy?
    a. The Act of Toleration
    b. The Stuart Act
    c. The Act of Succession
    d. The Stamp Act
    e. The Townshend Acts

Answer: c

2. The early Hanoverian kings spoke mainly
    a.   French.
    b.   English.
    c.   Dutch.
    d.   German.
    e.   Polish.

Answer: d

3. The Pragmatic Sanction
    a.   sought to forge a compromise between Protestants and Catholics.
    b.   sought to forge a compromise between Calvinists and Lutherans.
    c.   sought to ensure the right to succession of Maria Theresa.
    d.   sought to ensure the impartiality of courts in Prussia.
    e.   none of the above

Answer: c

4. The Seven Years'War was fought between which of the following years?
    a.   1732–1739
    b.   1714–1721
    c.   1763–1774
    d.   1777–1783
    e.   none of the above

Answer: e

5. Robert Clive made his name in
    a.   Quebec.
    b.   Prussia.
    c.   Kent.
    d.   India.
    e.   Delaware.

Answer: d

6. Poland was partitioned by
    a.   Russia, Prussia, and Austria.
    b.   Hungary, Russia, and Romania.
    c.   Hungary, Sweden, and Russia.
    d.   Ukraine, Austria, and Prussia.
    e.   Bohemia, Russia, and Prussia.

Answer: a

7. Eighteenth-century Whigs
   a. championed the rights of Parliament against the king.
   b. championed the rights of the king against Parliament.
   c. were the non-noble faction of the Tories.
   d. championed the rights of Catholics against Protestants.
   e. championed the rights of Protestants against Catholics.

Answer: a

8. Which of the following were prominent British radicals?
   a. Wilkes and Walpole
   b. Paine and Wilkes
   c. Paine and Pitt
   d. Burke and Paine
   e. Wilkes and North

Answer: b

9. The Treaty of Paris of 1763
   a. reflected Prussia's emergence as a Great Power.
   b. was a result of military and financial exhaustion.
   c. reflected widespread French defeats in North America.
   d. all of the above
   e. a and b only

Answer: d

10. Nobles in the Polish Parliament
    a. were weaker than the king.
    b. were tools of Prussian power.
    c. were tools of Austrian power.
    d. could veto any measure with a single member's vote.
    e. none of the above

Answer: d

Short-Answer Questions

1. What were the dynastic interests at play in the Seven Years' War?
2. How do we explain the fact that the kings of England in the early 1700s could barely speak English? What sorts of events had led to this state of affairs? Explain in detail.

3. Explain the difference between Whigs and Tories in eighteenth-century British politics.
4. What were some of the leading causes for the rise of nationalist sentiment in eighteenth-century Britain?
5. On what kinds of grounds were challenges against monarchical authority launched during the eighteenth century? Give concrete examples from at least three European countries.

True/False Questions

1. The War of the Austrian Succession began with the invasion of Pomerania by Frederick the Great.

Answer: F

2. With the professionalization of armies, mercenaries scarcely existed any longer by the end of the eighteenth century.

Answer: F

3. An important turning point in the history of India took place at Plassey in 1757.

Answer: T

4. Maria Theresa proved a strong and effective ruler.

Answer: T

5. Thomas Paine condemned the American Revolution.

Answer: F

6. The House of Commons grew to be stronger than the House of Lords in the eighteenth century.

Answer: T

7. The bayonet was a relatively new invention in warfare in the eighteenth century.

Answer: T

8. The South Sea Bubble resulted from the corruption of William Pitt.

Answer: F

9. The "Diplomatic Revolution" of 1756 saw a realignment of alliances, resulting in the linking of Britain and Prussia in an alliance.

Answer: T

10. After 1795, Poland vanished from the map of Europe.

Answer: T

Chronology

Place the following items in correct chronological order.
   9. Intolerable Acts
   3. War of Jenkins' Ear
   2. South Sea Bubble
   5. Seven Years' War begins
   4. Prussian invasion of Silesia
   8. Boston Tea Party
   7. First Partition of Poland
   6. Defeat of the French at Plassey
   1. Accession of George I to throne of England
  10. Reforms of Turgot

Part Four
Revolutionary Europe

Chapter 12
The French Revolution.

This chapter narrates the events of the French Revolution, starting with long-term origins, and ending with the rise to power of Napoleon. It traces the internal dynamics of power among the various revolutionary constituencies, the impact of war on the Revolution, and the institutional changes wrought by this upheaval.

Chapter Outline

I.   Popular sovereignty and nationalism

II. The Old Regime in crisis
    A. Long-term causes of the French Revolution
        1. Enlightenment ideas about legitimate rule
        2. Growing resentment of noble privileges
        3. Intransigent resistance by the privileged
        4. Economic hardship of the monarchy
        5. Remnants of feudal institutions
    B. The financial crisis
        1. Expensive wars
        2. Heavy indebtedness of the monarchy
        3. A rigid and inefficient fiscal system
        4. Louis XVI: a weak king
        5. Marie Antoinette: an unpopular queen
        6. Necker and Calonne: finance ministers under pressure
        7. An Assembly of Notables (1787) rejects fiscal reform

III. The first stages of the French Revolution
    A. Convoking the Estates-General
        1. The king faces a "revolt of the nobility"
        2. Voting within the Estates-General: a power struggle
        3. The self-assertion of the Third Estate: Abbé Sieyès

        4. The *cahiers de doléances*: a nationwide airing of grievances
        5. The Estates-General convenes at Versailles (May 5, 1789)
        6. Stalemate over voting procedures
        7. The Tennis Court Oath
        8. The king vainly seeks a compromise
    B. To the Bastille
        1. Rumors in Paris of a royal military plot
        2. Storming the symbolic fortress of despotism (July 14, 1789)
        3. A new government elected for Paris
    C. The Great Fear
        1. Peasants revolt in the provinces
        2. Abolition of the feudal regime (August 4, 1789)

IV. A new epoch
    A. Constitutional restraints upon the monarchy
    B. The Declaration of the Rights of Man and Citizen (August 26, 1789)
        1. Individual freedom
        2. Civic equality
        3. The primacy of reason
        4. Popular sovereignty
        5. Exclusion of women
        6. Religious freedom
    C. Growing pressure on the king
        1. Marat and the "patriots"
        2. Parisian women march on Versailles (October 5, 1789)
        3. The king and his family moved to Paris
    D. Reforming the Church
        1. Selling off Church lands (November 2, 1789)
        2. Civil Constitution of the Clergy: a national church
        3. Growth of a counter-revolutionary movement
    E. Structural reforms
        1. The Constitution of 1791: limited monarchy
        2. Restricted franchise
        3. Citizenship rights for Protestants and Jews
        4. Abolition of guilds
        5. Abolition of slavery in France (1791) and in colonies (1794)
        6. Olympe de Gouges and the rights of women
    F. The dynamics of radicalization
        1. Resistance to the Revolution
        2. Democratic clubs: the sans-culottes

          3.   The importance of symbols
     G.   The flight to Varennes
          1.   Louis XVI flees (June 20, 1791) and is returned to Paris

V.   War and its impact on the Revolution
     A.   Republican Jacobins
          1.   Danton
          2.   Marat
          3.   Robespierre
          4.   Taking control of the National Assembly by March 1792
     B.   Reactions throughout Europe
          1.   A profound threat to absolute monarchy everywhere
          2.   Burke's criticisms (1790) and Paine's defense (1791)
          3.   Mary Wollstonecraft's *Vindication of the Rights of Women* (1792)
          4.   The Declaration of Pilnitz (1791)
     C.   The National Assembly declares war on Austria (1792)
     D.   The Second Revolution
          1.   Early defeats in the war
          2.   A revolutionary Commune established in Paris (August 1792)
          3.   The September Massacres (1792)
          4.   The French victory at Valmy (September 1792)
          5.   The monarchy abolished (September 1792)
          6.   Success of the citizen-armies beyond France's borders
          7.   The king executed (January 21, 1793)
     E.   Quarrels and splits within the revolutionary leadership
          1.   Girondins: economic liberalism
          2.   Montagnards: radical centralizers
     F.   Counter-revolution
          1.   The role of the Church
          2.   The Vendée rebellion (March 1793)
     G.   The Terror
          1.   The Committee of Public Safety (March 1793)
          2.   Girondins vs. Jacobins
          3.   St. Just makes war on all "enemies of the Revolution"
          4.   Robespierre systematizes Jacobin power
          5.   Revolutionary symbols: a new calendar and Marianne
          6.   Between 11,000 and 18,000 deaths in the Terror
          7.   French military victories
          8.   The Revolution consumes its own children
          9.   The "Cult of the Supreme Being"

VI. The final stages
   A. Thermidor
      1. Robespierre guillotined (July 1794)
      2. Jacobins purged
   B. The Directory
      1. A new administrative body
      2. A turn against the asceticism of Robespierre
      3. Inflation
   C. Instability
      1. Failed royalist attempts to regain power
      2. Babeuf: a conspiracy of radical egalitarians
      3. The Directory moves toward full dictatorship
      4. Financial difficulties
      5. Napoleon's rising star
      6. The Treaty of Campo Formio (1797): French hegemony in Italy
      7. Russia, Britain, and Austria combine against Napoleon
      8. The coup d'état of Eighteenth Brumaire (November 9, 1799)

VII. Perspectives on the French Revolution
   A. Sweeping changes in the conquered territories
      1. Abolition of feudalism
      2. Weakening the Church
      3. Statemaking
      4. Indigenous nationalisms stimulated
   B. Historians' views of the Revolution
      1. The long influence of Marxist historians
      2. A bourgeois challenge to the Old Regime
      3. Critics of the Marxist interpretations
      4. The blurred lines of "bourgeoisie"
      5. Property versus status
      6. The thesis of the "Atlantic Revolution"
      7. Reforming tendencies already present under Old Regime
      8. A common conclusion: apprenticeship in modern democratic rule

Suggestions for Lecture Topics

For a lecture on the historiographical interpretations of the Revolution, see for instance Eric Hobsbawm, *Echoes from the Marseillaise*.

For a book that provides vivid narrative of the revolutionary period, written by an author highly critical of the revolutionaries, see Simon Schama, *Citizens*.

New historical approaches to the Revolution are exemplified in Lynn Hunt, *The Family Romance of the French Revolution*.

A classic study of the Revolution, worth a lecture in itself, is Alexis de Tocqueville's *Ancien Regime and the French Revolution*.

For a study of the military aspects of the revolutionary period, see Jean Paul Bertaud, *The Army of the French Revolution*.

Useful biographical portraits of revolutionary figures are provided in James M. Thompson, *Leaders of the French Revolution*.

Multiple-Choice Questions

1. Which of the following was NOT a Jacobin?
   a. Danton
   b. Marat
   c. De Gouges
   d. Robespierre
   e. St. Just

Answer: c

2. Which of the following was NOT a basic cause of the Revolution?
   a. Enlightenment ideas about legitimate rule
   b. growing resentment of nobles' privileges
   c. excessive wealth in the monarchy's treasury
   d. a weak king
   e. the intransigence of the nobles and clergy

Answer: c

3. The *cahiers de doléances* were:
   a. lists of grievances
   b. lists of potential traitors
   c. lists of priests
   d. lists of rights demanded by women
   e. none of the above

Answer: a

4. The First, Second, and Third Estates were
   a. the king, the clergy, and the nobles.
   b. the king, the clergy and nobles, and the bourgeoisie.
   c. the king and clergy, the nobles, and everyone else.
   d. the clergy, the nobles, and everyone else.
   e. the nobles, the bourgeoisie, and everyone else.

Answer: d

5. The author of an important pamphlet on the Third Estate was
   a. Robespierre.
   b. Sieyès.
   c. Danton.
   d. De Gouges.
   e. Marat.

Answer: b

6. Robespierre died
   a. under the guillotine.
   b. after being stabbed in his bathtub.
   c. in the revolutionary wars.
   d. of old age, in his bed.
   e. none of the above

Answer: a

7. The wars of the Revolution
   a. were fought to export the Revolution throughout Europe.
   b. were fought to defend the Revolution from external aggression.
   c. resulted in substantial victories for France.
   d. b and c only
   e. a, b, and c are all true.

Answer: e

8. The Civil Constitution of the Clergy
   a. was accompanied by the sale of indulgences.
   b. was accompanied by the sale of Church lands.
   c. abolished the Catholic Church in France.
   d. forced priests to proclaim personal allegiance to Robespierre.
   e. none of the above

Answer: b

9. The Eighteenth Brumaire was
   a. Napoleon's favorite horse.
   b. Napoleon's favorite ship.
   c. Napoleon's favorite regiment.
   d. a coup d'état launched against the Directory.
   e. a coup d'état launched against Robespierre.

Answer: d

10. The name of the Vendée is associated primarily with
    a. the square in Paris where the guillotine was located.
    b. a particularly radical Jacobin Club.
    c. a battle lost by the revolutionaries against the Dutch.
    d. counter-revolutionary rebellion.
    e. a region in which priests supported the Revolution.

Answer: d

Short-Answer Questions

1. What were the principal long-term causes of the French Revolution?
2. What were the principal short-term causes of the French Revolution?
3. Was the French Revolution "inevitable"? Whatever your answer, support your argument with plenty of concrete evidence from the chapter.
4. Some historians have argued that the internal dynamics of the Revolution led almost inexorably toward the Terror. Other historians disagree. Which side seems more convincing to you? Explain.
5. Describe the impact of foreign wars on the course of the Revolution.
6. What was the significance of the symbolic dimensions of the Revolution, such as the new calendar, the figure of Marianne, and the "Cult of Reason"?

True/False Questions

1. Necker was a popular general.

Answer: F

2. Talleyrand was guillotined in 1793.

Answer: F

3. The Declaration of the Rights of Man and Citizen included a provision for the freeing of slaves.

Answer: F

4. The Declaration of the Rights of Man and Citizen did not include guarantees for the rights of women.

Answer: T

5. Edmund Burke vigorously criticized the Revolution.

Answer: T

6. The Girondins were relative moderates.

Answer: T

7. Babeuf believed in the natural hierarchy of social orders.

Answer: F

8. The Treaty of Campo Formio reinstated Church authority in France.

Answer: F

9. The Committee of Public Safety never wielded real power.

Answer: F

10. Louis XVI almost succeeded in fleeing from France.

Answer: T

Chronology

Place the following items in correct chronological order.

10. Eighteenth Brumaire coup
4. Selling of Church lands
9. Treaty of Campo Formio
7. The Vendée rebellion
1. Assembly of Notables rejects Louis XVI's attempts at fiscal reform
2. Estates-General meet
3. Storming of the Bastille
6. Louis XVI executed
5. Louis XVI flees
8. Robespierre executed

Chapter 13
Napoleon and Europe

This chapter traces the rise and fall of Napoleon Bonaparte, paying particularly close attention to the long-lasting structural and institutional changes wrought upon France and much of Europe by this extraordinary man and the forces he unleashed.

Chapter Outline

I. Napoleon: heir or undertaker of the French Revolution?

II. Napoleon's rise to power
    A. Early years in Corsica
        1. Family origins in Lombardy
        2. Early military studies
    B. The Revolution
        1. Napoleon as a young Jacobin
        2. Putting down a royalist uprising (1795)
        3. Commander of the Army of Italy (1796)
        4. The Egyptian fiasco
        5. Eighteenth Brumaire

III. Consolidation of power
    A. The Consulat (1799)
        1. Plebiscite
        2. Stability
        3. Censorship
    B. The Concordat
        1. A compromise advantageous to both sides
        2. The Organic Articles
        3. State protection for non-Catholics
    C. Leadership style
    D. Wars

      1. The Treaty of Lunéville (1801)
      2. Inroads along the Rhine
      3. Becoming emperor of the French (1804)
      4. The sale of the Louisiana Territory (1803)
      5. The Third Coalition: Russia, Austria, and Britain (1805)
      6. The English victory at Trafalgar (1805)
      7. The crushing French victory at Austerlitz (1805)
      8. Dissolving the Holy Roman Empire (1806)
      9. Victory over Prussia at Jena (1806)
      10. Defeating the Russians at Friedland (1807)
      11. The Treaty of Tilsit (1807) punishes Prussia
      12. A renewed victory over Austria at Wagram (1809)
      13. The largest empire since the Roman Empire
   E. The Corsican warrior
      1. Turning eighteenth-century innovations to his best advantage
      2. The *levée en masse*, creating citizen-armies
      3. Harnessing the power of nationalism
      4. A logistical genius
      5. Meritocratic promotion in the French Army
      6. Rapid movement on the battlefield
      7. Loyalty
      8. A reign characterized by incessant warfare

IV. The French empire
   A. Imperial centralization
      1. Efficient administration
      2. The Bank of France (1800)
      3. Higher education at state expense
   B. The Napoleonic Code
      1. The Civil Code of 1804: perhaps the most lasting legacy
      2. Uniform laws for France
      3. Equality before the law
      4. Freedom of religion
      5. The family as social foundation
      6. Women and children subordinated
      7. Exportation of the Code to many parts of Europe
   C. The imperial hierarchy
      1. Ending legal barriers to social mobility
      2. The army and bureaucracy: pillars of empire
      3. The Legion of Honor

V. The tide turns against Napoleon
   A. The Continental System
      1. Strangling the British economy
      2. The British hold on
      3. Resentment of the blockade on the continent
   B. The Peninsular War in Spain (1807–1810)
      1. The hostility of the Spanish Church to French reforms
      2. Guerilla warfare
   C. The French presence stirs up European nationalisms
      1. The subordination of local interests to French interests
      2. Growing national sentiment in Germany: a thirst for unity
   D. Military reforms
      1. Prussia emulates the French system
   E. Decline of the empire
      1. Seeking an heir
      2. Dissent within France
      3. Megalomania
   F. War with Russia (1812)
      1. The costly advance to Moscow
      2. The disastrous winter retreat
      3. Out of 600,000, only 40,000 return to France
   G. Facing a four-power coalition
      1. The Battle of the Nations at Leipzig (1813)
      2. Paris captured in 1814; Napoleon abdicates

VI. Monarchical restoration and Napoleon's return
   A. The Treaty of Fontainebleau (1814)
      1. Restoration of monarchy: Louis XVIII
      2. Napoleon exiled to Elba
   B. The Bourbon Restoration
      1. A generous peace, thanks to Talleyrand's diplomacy
      2. The principle of representative government accepted by Louis XVIII
      3. The Code Napoléon stands
   C. The Hundred Days
      1. Napoleon's escape (March 1815)
      2. France rallies again behind the emperor; royalists flee
      3. Devastating defeat at Waterloo (June 1815)
      4. Exile to St. Helena and death six years later (1821)

VII. Napoleon's legacy

A. Consolidating and exporting the gains of the Revolution
B. Wars deadly to one Frenchman in five
C. A lasting mythology

Suggestions for Lecture Topics

For a lecture on the biographical details of this remarkable man's life, see Georges Lefebvre, *Napoleon*.

For a study of Napoleon's military campaigns, see Owen Connelly, *Blundering to Glory.*

An unusual angle on Napoleon's campaign in Russia, which makes for amusing and vivid material for a lecture, is Leo Tolstoy, *War and Peace.*

For an assessment of Napoleon's broader impact on Europe, see Stuart Woolf, *Napoleon's Integration of Europe.*

A vivid account of one turning point in Napoleon's career is given in Alan Schom, *Trafalgar.*

Multiple-Choice Questions

1. The Battle of Trafalgar was won by
    a. the French.
    b. the British.
    c. the Prussians.
    d. the Spaniards.
    e. the Austrians.

Answer: b

2. Which of the following was the location for a battle that represented a major defeat for France?
    a. Austerlitz
    b. Jena
    c. Friedland
    d. Wagram
    e. Leipzig

Answer: e

3. Which of the following was NOT a decisive factor in determining the superior effectiveness of Napoleon's armies?
    a. ample funding

  b. loyal troops
  c. nationalist sentiment
  d. rapid movement on the battlefield
  e. Napoleon's logistical brilliance

Answer: a

4. Which of the following was NOT a part of Napoleon's new legal code of 1804?
  a. special laws tailored for each region of France
  b. equality before the law
  c. freedom of religion
  d. the subordination of women and children to the male "head of household"
  e. ending legal barriers to social mobility

Answer: a

5. The Continental System
  a. was a uniform legal system applied by Napoleon to conquered territories.
  b. was a uniform administrative structure for all of Europe.
  c. called for the imposition of French as a language in all Europe.
  d. was designed to strangle Britain through economic isolation.
  e. none of the above

Answer: d

6. The Peninsular War in Spain
  a. brought Napoleon much-needed booty.
  b. crippled British power in the Mediterranean.
  c. bogged down Napoleon in a long and fruitless guerilla conflict.
  d. led to Napoleon's decline and fall.
  e. was won by Napoleon through the support of the Catholic Church.

Answer: c

7. Military officers in Napoleon's army could be:
  a. nobles.
  b. bourgeois.
  c. peasants and factory workers.
  d. all of the above
  e. a and b only

Answer: d

8. Louis XVI was succeeded on the throne by Louis XVIII, who was
   a. his son.
   b. his grandson.
   c. his brother.
   d. his uncle.
   e. none of the above

Answer: c

9. The peace terms after Napoleon's defeat in 1814 were
   a. very harsh for France.
   b. very generous for France.
   c. dictated by the fear of Napoleon's possible return.
   d. very harsh for France and for Italy.
   e. dictated by the religious conviction of Tsar Alexander.

Answer: b

10. Napoleon died at
    a. Waterloo.
    b. Elba.
    c. Paris.
    d. St. Helena.
    e. none of the above

Answer: d

Short-Answer Questions

1. Was Napoleon the heir or the undertaker of the French Revolution? Whatever your answer, provide plenty of concrete evidence to back up your argument.
2. What renders Napoleon famous to this day? What long-lasting changes did he bring to Europe?
3. What administrative and legal changes did Napoleon institute in France?
4. Why did the tide turn against Napoleon? What factors accounted for his downfall?
5. What distinguished Napoleon as a military leader? Was it just luck, or did he have specific leadership qualities? Explain.

True/False Questions

1. Napoleon was not born on the mainland of France.

Answer: T

2. Napoleon strongly opposed censorship.

Answer: F

3. Napoleon created the Bank of France.

Answer: T

4. Napoleon created a nationwide educational system for France.

Answer: T

5. Napoleon's only major defeat on land was at Waterloo.

Answer: F

6. St. Helena is an island in the Mediterranean.

Answer: F

7. The Concordat was a major treaty with the Holy Roman emperor.

Answer: F

8. The Treaty of Fontainebleau restored the monarchy to France.

Answer: T

9. Some aspects of Napoleon's legal code survived into the twentieth century.

Answer: T

10. Napoleon believed in the equality of women.

Answer: F

Chronology

Place the following items in correct chronological order.
    10. Napoleon's death
     5. Battle of Trafalgar
     4. Promulgation of the Civil Code

2. Eighteenth Brumaire coup d'état
1. Napoleon first assumes command of the Army of Italy
8. Napoleon's exile to the island of Elba
9. Battle of Waterloo
6. Treaty of Tilsit
7. Failed invasion of Russia
3. Sale of Louisiana Territory

Chapter 14
Challenges to Restoration Europe

This chapter describes the social and political tensions that pitted conservatives against the forces of liberalism and nationalism throughout Europe in the years following the defeat of Napoleon.

Chapter Outline

I. A protracted struggle between conservatives and new agencies of change
   A. New liberal and national movements

II. The post-Napoleonic settlement
   A. Restoring the balance of power
   B. The Treaty of Paris (May 1814)
      1. Talleyrand skillfully exploits tensions among the allies
      2. Rationale for a generous peace treaty
      3. No financial indemnity imposed
   C. The Congress of Vienna
      1. Four major players: Austria, Prussia, Britain, and Russia
      2. The dominant role of Klemens von Metternich
      3. The Holy Alliance: Prussia, Russia, and Austria
      4. Britain's Castlereagh pushes freedom of the seas
   D. The Congress System
      1. Balance of power as a guiding principle
      2. The fate of Poland
      3. Prussian gains
      4. The irrelevance of public opinion
      5. Adjustments in the Netherlands and Italy
      6. Creation of the German Confederation (1815)
   E. The Concert of Europe
      1. Weaknesses of Metternich's Austria

III. Restoration Europe

    A. The return of monarchs, nobles, and clergy
1. Attempts to turn back the clock
2. Continued power of the nobility, particularly in Eastern Europe
3. Nobles continue to dominate European military institutions
4. A religious revival

    B. Conservative ideology
1. Concepts of society as an organic unity: De Bonald
2. De Maistre: the crucial role of the Church
3. Conservative aspects of romanticism
4. Chateaubriand and *The Genius of Christianity* (1802)
5. Herder and the German *Sturm und Drang*: national community
6. A conflation of reform and revolution

IV. Stirrings of revolt

    A. Liberal movements
1. The Enlightenment heritage
2. Expansion of franchise
3. Civil liberties
4. Dis-establishment of the Church
5. Constitutional government
6. Strength in the West
7. Political organizations forming

    B. Uprisings in Spain, Portugal, and Italy
1. King Ferdinand VII of Spain rejects liberal constitution
2. Rebellions in Spanish colonies after 1816
3. Insurrection in Spain and Portugal (1820)
4. Italian secret societies: the Carbonari
5. Austrian troops crush revolts in Italy (1820–1821)
6. French troops crush Spanish rebels (1823)
7. Monroe Doctrine defends political changes in Americas (1823)

    C. Liberal movements in Germany
1. A convergence of liberalism and nationalism
2. Student fraternities, or *Burschenschaften*
3. Metternich clamps down with the Carlsbad Decrees

    D. The Greek revolt
1. Great-Power interests clash in the Mediterranean
2. Legitimacy of Ottoman rule vs. religious antagonism
3. Ypsilantis leads revolt against Ottoman rule (1821)
4. Byron and Shelley rally to the cause
5. The massacre of Chios (1821)

      6.   Treaty of Adrianople (1829):Turkish power recedes
- E. The Decembrist Revolt in Russia
  1.   Tsar Alexander I: initially in favor of reform
  2.   A polarized society
  3.   Alexander waxes reactionary after 1815
  4.   The new Tsar, Nicholas I, crushes a liberal conspiracy (1825)

V. The Bourbon restoration in France
- A. A constitutional monarchy
  1.   Restricted franchise
  2.   Modest freedoms
  3.   A return to Church influence
- B. The Ultra-royalists
  1.   Launching a "White Terror"
  2.   No compromise with regicides
  3.   The assassination of the duke of Berry (1820)
  4.   Birth of an heir, the count of Chambord
  5.   The transition to the reign of Charles X (1824)
  6.   Turning back the clock in France
- C. The Revolution of 1830
  1.   Resistance to the Restoration
  2.   Victor Hugo champions the forces of change
  3.   Stirrings of discontent against Charles X
  4.   The July Ordinances (1830): severe clampdown
  5.   Louis-Philippe, Orléanist leader, becomes king
  6.   A "bourgeois monarchy"
  7.   An end to noble privilege in politics
  8.   Guizot, prime minister: "Enrich yourselves!"
  9.   Between Legitimists and Republicans
  10. Louis-Philippe survives various plots

VI. Liberal assaults on the old order
- A. Belgium
  1.   A rebellion in Brussels against Dutch rule (1830)
  2.   A new constitutional monarchy is born (1831)
- B. Switzerland
  1.   The Congress of Vienna's legacy
  2.   Liberalizing reforms announced (1830)
  3.   War of the Sonderbund (1847)

VII. Nationalist struggles

    A. The revolt in Poland
        1. Russian domination
        2. Liberal–nationalist insurrection (1830–1831)
        3. Poles, divided among themselves, crushed by Russian troops
    B. Italy and Spain
        1. Italy: chafing under Austrian domination
        2. Liberals agitate for change
        3. Mazzini's ideal of a European confederation of nations
        4. Artists and composers support the cause of independence
        5. Spain's civil war over succession (1833)
    C. German nationalism
        1. The Vormärz
        2. Between liberal ideals and the quest for a strong state
        3. A weak tradition of individual liberties
        4. Particularism in a fragmented land
        5. The Zollverein, or customs union (1834)
        6. Liberalism as laissez-faire rather than political reform

VIII. Crisis and compromise in Britain
    A. Massacre at St. Peter's Fields (1819)
    B. Hunger and unemployment among the poor
    C. Religious and electoral reform
        1. Tories reluctantly open to compromise
        2. The Catholic Emancipation Act (1829)
        3. Whigs seeking electoral reform
    D. The Reform Bill of 1832
        1. Influence of the French Revolution of 1830
        2. The intransigeance of the House of Lords
        3. A compromise solution: a moderate move toward democracy
        4. Campaigns against slavery and child labor
    E. The repeal of the Corn Laws
        1. Tariffs on imported grain keep prices high
        2. Liberals seek free trade reforms
        3. Prime Minister Robert Peel sees through repeal of tariffs
    F. Chartism
        1. A "Great Charter" on behalf of democratization
        2. The largest working-class movement in the century
        3. Parliamentary rejections (1839 and 1842)

Suggestions for Lecture Topics

For a superb account of the early formation of working-class movements and consciousness in Britain, see E.P. Thompson, *The Making of the English Working Class*. For a lecture on Chartism see James Epstein, *The Lion of Freedom*.

For a lecture on the changing roles of women during this period see Priscilla Smith Robertson, *An Experience of Women*.

An interesting sociological work on shifting patterns of legitimacy during this period is Reinhard Bendix, *Kings or People?*.

David Pinckney's *The French Revolution of 1830* provides an excellent account of that event, suitable for drawing material for lectures. Students may also be drawn to study this event by linking it with the popular musical, *Les Misérables*, a viewing of which in video form might provide a fine opportunity for comparing historical and artistic representations of the same event.

On early German nationalism see Walter Laqueur, *Young Germany*. On Italian nationalism see Harry Hearder, *Italy in the Age of the Risorgimento*.

Multiple-Choice Questions

1. Which of the following was NOT a major player at the Congress of Vienna?
   a. France
   b. Prussia
   c. Britain
   d. Russia
   e. Italy

Answer: e

2. The Holy Alliance included
   a. France, Italy, Austria.
   b. Austria, Prussia, Russia.
   c. Austria, Russia, France.
   d. Austria, Prussia, England.
   e. Austria, Russia, England.

Answer: b

3. The words *Sturm und Drang* mean
   a. Storm and Stress.
   b. Storm and Tide.
   c. Flight and Hope.
   d. Home and Hearth.
   e. Poetry and Soul.

Answer: a

4. Which of the following was NOT a conservative?
   a. De Maistre
   b. De Bonald
   c. Metternich
   d. Mazzini
   e. Burke

Answer: d

5. The Decembrist Revolt was undertaken by
   a. Prussian military officials.
   b. Russian peasants.
   c. Scottish nobles.
   d. Russian military officers.
   e. Austrian Catholics.

Answer: d

6. Mazzini believed that
   a. nations were natural.
   b. Italy's destiny was to recreate the Roman Empire.
   c. war among nations was unavoidable.
   d. all of the above
   e. a and c only

Answer: a

7. Charles X was
   a. a moderate.
   b. a reactionary.
   c. a reformer.
   d. an atheist.
   e. a liberal.

Answer: b

8. The Carbonari were
   a.   elite troops.
   b.   Spanish merchants.
   c.   an Italian secret society.
   d.   Greek patriots.
   e.   none of the above

Answer: c

9. The Congress of Vienna was dominated by
   a.   Talleyrand.
   b.   Tsar Alexander.
   c.   Castlereagh.
   d.   Mazzini.
   e.   none of the above

Answer: e

10. The Zollverein was
    a.   a nationalist student fraternity.
    b.   a repressive law passed by Metternich.
    c.   a widely read book.
    d.   a customs union.
    e.   none of the above

Answer: d

Short-Answer Questions

1. What were the underlying ideological principles of the Restoration? What ideas did intellectuals like Burke and De Maistre use to defend the principles of "legitimacy" and royal prerogative?
2. What were the meanings of the word "liberalism" in the first half of the nineteenth century? How do these meanings differ from the meanings often ascribed to this word in the late twentieth century?
3. Why were liberalism and nationalism often linked together in the minds of many people in the early nineteenth century?
4. What was the Holy Alliance, and why did Britain and France refuse to participate in it?
5. Why did Britain avert revolution in 1830 and yet again in 1848, when so many parts of Europe experienced upheaval and turmoil during these years? What factors made Britain different?

True/False Questions

1. The duke of Berry left no heir after his death.

Answer: F

2. Talleyrand was a skillful general.

Answer: F

3. The *Sturm und Drang* was an artistic movement infused with nationalist sentiment.

Answer: T

4. Louis-Philippe was known as the "July King."

Answer: F

5. The *Sonderbund* took shape in Switzerland.

Answer: T

6. The *Vormärz* is Austria's national anthem.

Answer: F

7. *The Genius of Christianity* was written by Chateaubriand.

Answer: T

8. Belgium first became an independent country in 1831.

Answer: T

9. Castlereagh was killed in a duel.

Answer: F

10. Chios was the site of a Turkish massacre of Greeks.

Answer: T

Chronology

Place the following items in correct chronological order.
    3. Massacre of Chios
    7. Belgium's independence

1. Congress of Vienna
4. Monroe Doctrine
6. Decembrist Revolt
8. Great Reform Bill passed
10. Zollverein created
9. Birth of the July Monarchy
5. Beginning of reign of Charles X
2. Austrian troops crush Italian liberal rebellions

Chapter 15
The Middle Classes in the Era of Liberalism

This chapter describes the social, political, and economic aspects of the rise to increasing prominence of the middle classes in much of Europe during the first half of the nineteeth century. It describes the middle-class way of life, middle-class attitudes, and the cultural and artistic creations that characterized this period.

Chapter Outline

I.   Diversity of the middle classes
    A.   Etymology of "bourgeois" from the Middle Ages
    B.   A broad range of economic situations and social status
        1.   The wealthiest
        2.   The "petty bourgeoisie," dreaming of upward mobility
    C.   Variations in bourgeois Europe
        1.   A tendency to invest in land rather than in business
        2.   Britain's landed elite
        3.   Merchants and lawyers on the continent
        4.   Eastern Europe: middle classes weak and small
    D.   Social mobility
        1.   Commerce seen as a positive moral force
        2.   James Mill's denunciation of noble privilege (1820)
        3.   "Respectability": middle-class honor
        4.   The "self-made man"
    E.   The rising professions
        1.   Lawyers: rising in respectability
        2.   Medicine: a rapidly growing profession
        3.   The British Medical Act (1858): standardized credentials
        4.   State officials and bureaucrats

II. Middle-class culture
   A. Primacy of the family
      1. Choosing a marriage partner
      2. Contraception
      3. Developing concepts of childhood and adolescence
   B. Separate spheres
      1. A woman's status linked to that of her father and husband
      2. Restrictions on legal rights
      3. Looking after the domestic world
      4. Early feminists: Harriet Taylor Mill's *The Enfranchisement of Women*
      5. Early anti-feminists
   C. A culture of comfort
      1. Private spheres and prosperity
      2. New appurtenances appear in bourgeois homes
      3. Developing social segregation in the cities
      4. A boom in the sale of books and newspapers
      5. Travel for pleasure
   D. Education
      1. Secondary education provides a common cultural background
      2. Growing universities
      3. Education restricted primarily to elites
      4. Middle-class reformers' faith in education as social healer
   E. Religion
      1. Faith and "respectability"
      2. Sunday schools for the working classes
      3. Secularized education expands
   F. Public service
      1. The expansion of charities
      2. Voluntary associations grapple with impact of industrialization

III. Liberalism and its ambiguities
   A. The franchise
      1. Replacing the "rights of man" with the "rights of citizen"
      2. Seeking a broader franchise (but not universal suffrage)
   B. Liberals and laissez-faire
      1. Non-intervention by the state
      2. Adam Smith's teachings held up as a standard
      3. Bentham's utilitarianism: "greatest good for greatest number"
      4. Ricardo's "iron law of wages"

        5.   Liberals seek restrictions on workingmans' organizations
   C. State intervention
        1.   Repression of the lower orders
        2.   Reforming liberals turn to government as their instrument
        3.   Anti-slavery crusades
        4.   Education for the poor
        5.   J. S. Mill: government's positive role in social reform

IV. Romanticism
   A. Literature and painting
        1.   Reacting against Enlightenment rationalism
        2.   The legacy of Rousseau and German idealism
        3.   Coleridge and Wordsworth's "new poetry"
        4.   The power of nature
        5.   Unleashing the senses and the passion of the soul
        6.   Goethe's Faust: the outsider as hero
   B. Music
        1.   Beethoven: defying traditional harmonies and structures
        2.   Exploring the intricacies of the subjective world
        3.   Public concerts growing in popularity

Suggestions for Lecture Topics

Students tend to enjoy, and profit from, a slide show on romantic art. One of the best ways to carry this out is to place two projectors side by side and have the students themselves elicit the differences between the neoclassical style of the Enlightenment and romantic works of the early nineteenth century.

Similarly, a reading from romantic poetry, such as Wordsworth's *Tintern Abbey*, makes for an absorbing lecture. Students are usually intrigued when one points out some of the points of similarity (and the differences) between the turn to nature that occurred during the early nineteenth century and the turn to nature that occurred much more recently, during the 1960s' counterculture.

A magnificent work from which to draw material for lectures is Peter Gay, *The Bourgeois Experience*.

An excellent work on romanticism is Meyer Abrams, *The Mirror and the Lamp*.

A lecture on John Stuart Mill provides a good focus for discussion of liberalism. See Bernard Semmel, *John Stuart Mill and the Pursuit of Virtue*.

Multiple-Choice Questions

1. Which of the following is the etymological root of the word "bourgeois"?
   a. bourg, meaning mountain
   b. bourg, meaning rich
   c. bourg, meaning town.
   d. bourgeois, meaning vulgar.
   e. none of the above

Answer: c

2. The author of *The Enfranchisement of Women* was
   a. J. S. Mill.
   b. J. S. Mill's wife.
   c. J. S. Mill's mother.
   d. J. S. Mill's daughter.
   e. J. S. Mill's son.

Answer: b

3. As he grew older, J. S. Mill
   a. became more concerned with the plight of the poor.
   b. became less concerned with the plight of the poor.
   c. became a socialist.
   d. became a conservative.
   e. none of the above

Answer: a

4. Which of the following was most closely associated with the philosophy
   of utilitarianism?
   a. Smith
   b. Ricardo
   c. Mill
   d. Bentham
   e. Peel

Answer: d

5. Goethe wrote:
   a. *On Poetry.*
   b. *On the Emancipation of Women.*
   c. *Faust.*
   d. both a and c

   e.   none of the above

Answer: c

6. Ricardo's "iron law of wages" stipulated that
   a.   people would always seek to earn more than they did.
   b.   inflation was unavoidable.
   c.   wages, left to market forces, would rise steadily.
   d.   wages, left to market forces, would fall to subsistence levels.
   e.   none of the above

Answer: d

7. Romantic art
   a.   tended to avoid nature.
   b.   tended toward rational representations of nature.
   c.   depicted the Industrial Revolution.
   d.   depicted mainly love stories.
   e.   depicted nature frequently.

Answer: e

8. Liberals in the first half of the nineteenth century sought
   a.   universal suffrage.
   b.   a broader franchise, but not universal suffrage.
   c.   a narrower franchise.
   d.   all of the above at different times
   e.   none of the above

Answer: b

9. The middle classes were
   a.   larger in Western Europe than in Eastern Europe.
   b.   smaller in Western Europe than in Eastern Europe.
   c.   growing, but still smaller than the nobility in the year 1850.
   d.   not growing, but staying about the same size.
   e.   none of the above

Answer: a

10. Most liberals
   a.   accepted the workers' right to unionize.
   b.   rejected the workers' right to unionize.
   c.   believed that working-class women should unionize.
   d.   believed that children should be paid a fixed rate.

e.   felt that most workers were not being paid enough.

Answer: b

Short-Answer Questions

1. What was new and different about the middle-class presence in European society in the nineteenth century, as compared with previous centuries? Describe the social, economic, and political aspects of this question.
2. This chapter describes the ambiguities of nineteenth-century liberal thought, ambiguities that centered around the three principal issues of the franchise, state intervention in the economy, and social reform. Describe and discuss these three ambiguous areas of liberal thought.
3. What was the condition of middle-class women in nineteenth-century Europe? Was it true that their lot was a completely powerless one, or were there ways in which they could assert their will, despite their legal and social subordination to men?
4. In what ways did romanticism differ from the artistic currents that had characterized the Enlightenment?
5. What did it mean to be a "liberal" in nineteenth-century Europe? What ideals would a liberal support, and what principles would a liberal oppose?

True/False Questions

1. The etymology of the word "bourgeois" can be traced to ancient Rome.

Answer: F

2. John Stuart Mill wrote *The Enfranchisement of Women*.

Answer: F

3. Most nineteenth-century liberals sought universal suffrage for men and women.

Answer: F

4. Most nineteenth-century liberals sought universal suffrage for males.

Answer: F

5. Beethoven became deaf halfway through his career as a composer.

Answer: T

6. The Falloux Law in France restored Catholic Church authority in supervising schools.

Answer: T

7. The British Medical Act required doctors not to turn away any sick person who presented himself or herself for treatment.

Answer: F

8. Contraception began to be widely practiced in parts of Europe during this period.

Answer: T

9. *Faust* was written by Schiller.

Answer: F

10. The "bobbies," a nickname for unarmed English policemen, comes from the name of Robert Peel.

Answer: T

Chronology

Place the following items in correct chronological order.

    5. James Stuart Mill publishes *An Essay on Government*
    9. British Medical Act
    8. Harriet Taylor Mill publishes *The Enfranchisement of Women*
    6. Chartist campaigns
    4. Ricardo's *Principles of Political Economy and Taxation* published
    7. Falloux Law in France
    1. Adam Smith publishes *The Wealth of Nations*
    3. Coleridge's and Wordsworth's manifesto on the "new poetry"
  10. John Stuart Mill publishes *On Liberty*
    2. Goethe publishes *Faust*

Chapter 16
The Industrial Revolution, 1800–1850

This chapter relates the changes wrought by industrialization in Europe during the first half of the nineteenth century, and analyzes some of the major consequences for the socioeconomic and political order.

Chapter Outline

I.   A transformation in the way Europeans lived

II. Preconditions for transformation
   A. Historians' earlier emphasis on a sudden technological "take-off"
   B. New research showing long-term, gradual changes
   C. Demographic explosion
      1. Growing population in eighteenth century
      2. A new phenomenon, or part of an older cyclical pattern?
      3. Continued sources of disease
      4. Nevertheless a steadily declining mortality rate
      5. The 1800s: a century of relative peace
   D. The expanding agricultural base
      1. Accumulation of capital
      2. More land under cultivation
      3. Farm yields increasing
      4. The waning of the small family farm
      5. Productivity growing even in Eastern Europe (except Russia)
   E. Trains and steamboats
      1. A revolution in transportation
      2. England's first freight line (1820) and passenger line (1830)
      3. Private investment pours into English railroads
      4. Collateral effects of railways on metallurgical industries
      5. Burgeoning passenger service

      6. Steamship lines expanding throughout Europe

III. A variety of national industrial experiences
    A. Britain takes the lead
      1. Why did England industrialize first?
      2. Eighteenth-century manufacturing already well developed
      3. Coal and iron ore deposits
      4. Rich colonial trade
      5. Plenty of capital ready for investment
      6. A precocious system of financial instruments for investment
      7. An entrepreneurial ethic
      8. Cotton products: half of British exports through 1850s
    B. France: running in second place
      1. Coal resources less impressive than in Britain
      2. Obstacles to private investment
      3. A penchant for producing hand-crafted luxury items
      4. A greater role for state leadership than in Britain
    C. Germany: late and fast
      1. Germany lags behind until the mid-nineteenth century
      2. A fragmented, rural region
      3. Textiles, then Ruhr coal, launch the manufacturing wave
      4. The Zollverein (1834), brainchild of Friedrich List
      5. Alfred Krupp launches the German steel industry
    D. Southern and Eastern Europe
      1. A pattern of sparse industrialization
      2. Piedmont and Lombardy, Catalonia, Bohemia: rare exceptions
      3. Spain's weak infrastructures
      4. Russian transportation problems and hostility to the West

IV. Impact of the Industrial Revolution
    A. Continuities on the land
      1. The proliferation of landless laborers in Europe
      2. Machines taking away many jobs
      3. Captain Swing and machine breaking in Britain
      4. Rural conditions perhaps even worsening in Eastern Europe
    B. Urbanization
      1. Industrial towns, commercial and administrative centers grow
      2. Appalling industrial slums
      3. Urbanization slower and more sparse, the farther east one went
    C. Migration and mobility
      1. Moving from rural areas to cities in search of work

      2. The "Hungry Forties"

      3. Emigration to the United States and other regions

V. Industrial work

    A. Machine-breaking Luddites

    B. The moral indignation of Dickens at the industrial way of life

    C. Gender and family

      1. Women working in proportions similar to men

      2. Wage labor alters family life and mores

      3. Domestic service the largest category of female employment

      4. Textile mills the second-largest employers of females

      5. Balancing wage needs and child-rearing needs

      6. Prostitution

    D. Child labor

      1. Before the industrial era

      2. Low wages: about a quarter of an adult's

      3. Dangerous labor in factories

      4. The Factory Act of 1833 in Britain

      5. France's first child labor law (1841)

    E. The standard of living

      1. The grim face of unrestricted capitalism

      2. Appalling conditions of labor and life

      3. The "standard of living debate" among historians

      4. An increasing gap between rich and poor

      5. Bread as the central expenditure for many

      6. Extreme vulnerability of working families

      7. Housing conditions worse than in previous centuries

    F. Poor relief

      1. Paternalistic factory owners: the rare exception

      2. Britain's Speenhamland system (1795)

      3. The Poor Law Amendment Act (1834): workhouses

      4. Charitable institutions

    G. Class consciousness

      1. One source of identity among many

      2. Urban artisans and ancient hierarchies of skill

      3. The phenomenon of "de-skilling"

      4. Going beyond ancient trade divisions toward a common identity

    H. Workers' associations and social protest

      1. A new militancy

      2. Repeal of British Combination Acts (1824) spurs trade unions

      3. "Friendly societies" of workers

    4. The continuing illegality of strikes
    5. Artisans lead the way in movement of social protest
    6. A peak of protest in Britain between 1820 and 1850
    7. Methodism puts on the brakes
    8. Militancy in France and Germany

VI. The origins of European socialism
    A. Utopian socialists
        1. Dreams of a perfectly harmonious society
        2. Articulating a critique of liberal capitalism
        3. The "social question" forcefully raised
        4. Saint-Simon's "religion of humanity": a productivity hierarchy
        5. Fourier's phalansteries
        6. Robert Owen's experiments at New Lanark
        7. Cabet's fusion of Christianity and the "social question"
    B. Other early socialists
        1. Casting the bourgeoisie as nonproducers
        2. Flora Tristan's campaign for women's and workers' rights
        3. Louis Blanc posits the state as the agency of change (1839)
        4. Proudhon: "property is theft"
    C. Marx
        1. Hegel's vision of history as progress through logical stages
        2. From feudalism to capitalism to socialism: a necessary order
        3. The *Communist Manifesto* (1848)

Suggestions for Lecture Topics

E. P. Thompson's *The Making of the English Working Class* remains a master-piece of historical writing thirty years after its first publication (1964). It provides a rich source of material for lectures on the life and attitudes of workers during the early nineteenth century.

For a lecture on the conditions of life in industrial England, the descriptions provided in Friedrich Engels' *The Condition of the Working Class in England* make gripping accounts. For a contrasting view see Gertrude Himmelfarb, *Poverty and Compassion.*

Many students will find the technological aspects of the industrial transformation fascinating. For a detailed narration and analysis of the role of technology see David Landes, *The Unbound Prometheus.*

An interesting study of working-class associations in France is William Sewell, *Work and Revolution in France.*

The utopian socialists make excellent material for a lecture; their lives and ideas are deftly described in Frank Manuel, *The Prophets of Paris.*

A broad interpretive study of the themes discussed in this chapter is Barrington Moore, *Injustice.*

Multiple-Choice Questions

1. Population in the nineteenth century was
   a. rising.
   b. declining.
   c. holding steady.
   d. rising in the countryside and declining in the cities.
   e. rising in the countryside and holding steady in the cities.

Answer: a

2. Which of the following is NOT one of the major reasons why England industrialized first?
   a. rich iron and coal deposits
   b. an entrepreneurial ethic
   c. state-funded and subsidized railroads
   d. innovative banking and financial methods
   e. a rich colonial trade providing plenty of capital

Answer: c

3. Which nation was the next to industrialize after England?
   a. Germany
   b. Russia
   c. Spain
   d. the Netherlands
   e. France

Answer: e

4. Alfred Krupp was
   a. the creator of the Zollverein.
   b. an inventor.
   c. the industrial partner of Friedrich Engels.
   d. a steel manufacturer.
   e. a textiles manufacturer.

Answer: d

5. The Luddites were
   a.   a religious confraternity.
   b.   a workers' Methodist group.
   c.   a group of Manchester economists.
   d.   machine-breaking workers.
   e.   none of the above

Answer: d

6. Which of the following regions was NOT one of the exceptional
   pockets of advanced industrialization in Southern and Eastern Europe?
   a.   Piedmont
   b.   Lombardy
   c.   Calabria
   d.   Catalonia
   e.   Bohemia

Answer: c

7. The single largest source of employment for working-class women was
   a.   prostitution.
   b.   textiles.
   c.   farming.
   d.   domestic service.
   e.   none of the above

Answer: d

8. Children generally earned which proportion of an adult's wages?
   a.   a quarter
   b.   a half
   c.   a third
   d.   the same
   e.   a tenth

Answer: a

9. Strikes in many parts of early-nineteenth century Europe were
   a.   common.
   b.   illegal.
   c.   considered by most workers to be unfair to one's employer.
   d.   considered by most workers to be a sin.
   e.   an important part of the workers' repertoire of social protest.

Answer: b

10. Which of the following coined the term "phalanstery"?
    a.   Marx
    b.   Cabet
    c.   Owen
    d.   Saint-Simon
    e.   none of the above

Answer: e

Short-Answer Questions

1. Describe the major preconditions for the Industrial Revolution. What major aspects of European society were already in place, and what currents were already visible before the industrialization process got underway in England?
2. Why did England industrialize first? Describe at least four major factors that help account for this phenomenon.
3. What factors slowed down the industrialization process in France, Germany, and Russia?
4. What factors stood in the way of working-class individuals acquiring a sense of common identity, or "class consciousness"?
5. What was the difference between the vision put forward by the utopian socialists and Karl Marx? Discuss the thought of at least two utopian socialists in some detail, as well as the thought of Marx.

True/False Questions

1. Flora Tristan was Karl Marx's lover.

Answer: F

2. The child labor law of 1841 in France limited the legal work period for children between the ages of thirteen and sixteen to six days a week, twelve hours a day.

Answer: T

3. Speenhamland was the name of Robert Owen's experimental factory.

Answer: F

4. Friedrich List was the intellectual father of the Zollverein.

Answer: T

5. Cabet's utopia relied heavily on Christian principles.

Answer: T

6. Captain Swing was the constable who ordered a massacre of workers in 1819.

Answer: F

7. Marx published the *Communist Manifesto* in 1861.

Answer: F

8. Saint-Simon wanted to create a rigorously egalitarian society in which all hierarchy would be abolished.

Answer: F

9. Worker militancy was greater in France and Germany than in England.

Answer: T

10. England's first freight railroad line was opened in 1820.

Answer: T

Chronology

Place the following items in correct chronological order.

  2. Repeal of British Combination Acts
  3. England's first passenger train line
  5. Zollverein created
  1. Speenhamland system created
  8. *Communist Manifesto* published
  4. British Factory Act passed
10. Dickens published *Hard Times*
  6. Louis Blanc publishes *The Organization of Work*
  9. Crystal Palace exhibition in London
  7. Potato famine

Chapter 17
The Revolutions of 1848

This chapter describes the ferment of liberalism, nationalism, and socialism that swept through much of Europe in the Revolutions of 1848, the conflicting aims of the revolutionaries, and the counter-revolutions that followed.

Chapter Outline

I. Revolutionary mobilization
    A. The February Revolution in France
        1. Republicans organize banquets as rallying points for reform
        2. Workers demand broadening of franchise
        3. The insurrection of February 22, 1848
        4. Louis-Philippe abdicates; Second Republic proclaimed
        5. The political colors of the provisional government
        6. Universal manhood suffrage and abolition of slavery
        7. The revolution spreads through the provinces
        8. An economic crisis sets in
        9. National Workshops established for indigent workers
        10. Questioning the role of women
        11. New elections in April bring a conservative majority
    B. Revolution in the German states
        1. German liberals and radicals at odds
        2. News from France brings a flurry of revolts in Germany
        3. Shooting in Berlin kills 250 (March 18)
        4. A widespread ferment of political discussion
        5. Concessions from frightened rulers
    C. Revolution in Central Europe
        1. Czechs and Magyars seek increased independence
        2. Kossuth and the Hungarian liberals
        3. Clashes in Vienna (March 13): Metternich flees to England
        4. Emperor Ferdinand announces reforms, then balks

         5.   Hungarians assert complete autonomy from Vienna

         6.   Czech nationalists revolt in Prague

  D. The Italian states

         1.   Rebels animated by a plethora of differing goals

         2.   Revolt in Milan sparks nationalist tumult in all Italy

         3.   The Piedmontese march into Lombardy

         4.   The pope supports the Habsburgs

         5.   The Battle of Custoza (August 1848): a key Austrian victory

II. Quest for revolutionary consensus

  A. Crisis in France

         1.   Split between liberals and radicals

         2.   The National Assembly closes the National Workshops (June 23)

         3.   The "June Days": a bloody dénouement

         4.   Class lines blurred in the civil strife

         5.   Popular political movements banned

         6.   Louis Napoleon Bonaparte elected president (December 10, 1848)

  B. The Frankfurt Parliament

         1.   Paving the way for a liberal and national constitution

         2.   The Frankfurt Parliament meets (May 1848)

         3.   A parliament without a state

         4.   *Kleindeutsch* vs. *Grossdeutsch* solutions

         5.   Martial law imposed in Prussia

         6.   The Frankfurt Parliament's harsh vote on the Polish Question

         7.   Proclamation of Basic Rights of the German People (December 1848)

         8.   Prussia rejects the Parliament's offer of unification

         9.   The failure of the Frankfurt Parliament

III. Counter-revolution

  A. Liberal ideals vs. the "red scare"

  B. Central Europe

         1.   The different meanings of "freedom" to different people

         2.   Competing nationalist aims

         3.   Armies and cannon restore the status quo

         4.   The "Patent" of December 31, 1851: restoring absolutism in Vienna

         5.   The "Bach system" roots out political opposition

         6.   Showdown over Hungarian autonomy (April 14, 1849)

         7.   Russian intervention crushes Hungarian independence

        8.   Repression and reimposition of absolutism in the German states

  C. Prussian-Austrian rivalry

        1.   "Humiliation of Olmütz" (November 29, 1850): Prussian Union foiled

  D. Italy

        1.   Piedmont renews the war against Austria, then sues for peace

        2.   Revolt against the papacy in Rome

        3.   French troops restore papal authority

        4.   Venice capitulates to Austrian armies (August 1849)

  E. The French Second Republic

        1.   Louis Napoleon consolidates his hold

        2.   Strength of the left in many regions of the nation

        3.   Systematic governmental repression

        4.   The Falloux Law (1850) strengthens Catholic hold on education

        5.   Secret societies form in southern and central France

        6.   Louis Napoleon's coup of December 2, 1851

        7.   Ratification by plebiscite

        8.   Louis Napoleon, emperor of the French (1852)

IV. The legacy of 1848

  A. Strengthening of state institutions

  B. The pivotal role of professional armies

  C. Pioneering action by workers

  D. Apprenticeship for republicanism and nationalism in Germany and Italy

  E. The spread of liberal ideas throughout much of Europe

  F. In Germany, liberalism weakened and nationalism strengthened

  G. The staying power of a reformed Habsburg monarchy

  H. The conspicuous absence of Britain and Russia from the 1848 upheavals

Suggestions for Lecture Topics

For a lecture on France in 1848, see Maurice Agulhon, *The Republican Experiment*; John Merriman, *The Agony of the Republic*; and Ted Margadant, *French Peasants in Revolt*.

    The memoirs of Carl Schurz make for a gripping lecture on the atmosphere in Germany during the revolutionary period. On the revolutions in Germany, see Jonathan Sperber, *Rhineland Radicals*.

For a lecture on the revolutions in Italy, see Derek Beales, *The Risorgimento and the Unification of Italy.*

On the Austrian response to the insurrection, see Alan Sked, *The Survival of the Habsburg Empire.*

On the intellectual aspects of the revolutions, see the classic work by Lewis Namier, *The Revolution of the Intellectuals.*

Multiple-Choice Questions

1. The Revolutions of 1848 first broke out in
   a. Paris.
   b. Palermo.
   c. Vienna.
   d. Berlin.
   e. Frankfurt.

Answer: b

2. A key reason for the failure of the Revolutions of 1848 was
   a. insufficient funding.
   b. excessive military force at the outset.
   c. the weak demands of the leaders.
   d. divisions between liberals and radicals.
   e. all of the above

Answer: d

3. Metternich's response to the Revolutions of 1848 was
   a. to have the leaders executed.
   b. to have the leaders arrested.
   c. to flee to Italy.
   d. to urge the emperor to abdicate.
   e. to flee to England.

Answer: e

4. The *Kleindeutsch* versus *Grossdeutsch* solutions had to do with
   a. creating a unified Germany with or without Habsburg lands.
   b. creating a unified Prussia with or without Austrian help.
   c. creating a tariff union bigger or smaller than the Zollverein.
   d. creating a common German language based on that spoken in Berlin or Hamburg.
   e. none of the above

Answer: a

5. The "June Days" were
   a. the triumphant moment of the Frankfurt Parliament.
   b. the crushing of Hungarian independence by Russian armies.
   c. the defeat of Piedmont by Austria.
   d. the crushing of radical insurrection in Paris.
   e. the return of Louis Napoleon to power.

Answer: d

6. The "humiliation of Olmütz" was about
   a. the Prussian king refusing a "crown from the gutter."
   b. Austrian intrigue foiling the creation of a Prussian Union.
   c. the Prussian king's bad treatment by French diplomats.
   d. the refusal by the Prussian king's staff to give a glass of water to one of the representatives of the Frankfurt Parliament.
   e. none of the above

Answer: b

7. The French Falloux Law of 1850
   a. repressed social and political organizations.
   b. imposed a surtax on drink.
   c. subjected prostitutes to government inspection.
   d. retroactively legalized the candidacy of Louis Napoleon.
   e. none of the above

Answer: e

8. Which of the following was NOT part of the legacy of 1848?
   a. strengthening of state institutions
   b. making clear the importance of professional armies in state power
   c. German support for the independence of Poland
   d. liberalism weakened in Germany
   e. nationalism strengthened in Germany

Answer: c

9. In December 1851, Louis Napoleon
   a. took power legally, and a plebiscite confirmed this.
   b. took power illegally, but a plebiscite indicated public acceptance of this.
   c. faced massive insurrections in the provinces, which caused him to declare martial law.
   d. raised taxes, which increased his unpopularity.
   e. none of the above

Answer: b

10. The two powers most conspicuously absent from the tumult of 1848 were
    a. Turkey and Greece.
    b. Italy and Denmark.
    c. Russia and Spain.
    d. England and Russia.
    e. England and Czechoslovakia.

Answer: d

Short-Answer Questions

1. What was the primary source of tension between liberals and radicals in France and Germany during the Revolutions of 1848?
2. What precipitated the Revolutions of 1848? Describe both the short-term and the longer-term causes of upheaval.
3. What precipitated the June Days in Paris? Describe the major factions that faced each other as enemies during this confrontation, and the consequences of their conflict.
4. Describe the tension between liberalism and nationalism in the German states, and its role in determining the fate of the Frankfurt Parliament.
5. What was the legacy of the Revolutions of 1848? Were these revolutions merely a "tale of sound and fury, signifying nothing," or did they (despite their failures) bring about lasting changes in European society? Explain.

True/False Questions

1. The Falloux Law was a victory for the Catholic Church.

Answer: T

2. The death of Metternich helped fuel the hopes of the 1848 revolutionaries in Vienna.

Answer: F

3. The June Days ended in total defeat for the radical insurgents.

Answer: T

4. Louis Napoleon held power after 1851 as a virtual dictator of France.

Answer: T

5. Louis Napoleon was elected president in 1848 by a majority of French citizens in a free election.

Answer: T

6. Louis Napoleon was the grandson of Napoleon Bonaparte.

Answer: F

7. The "Bach system" was a new form of musical notation.

Answer: F

8. Every major nation in Europe, with the exception of Britain and Russia, experienced the revolutionary upheavals of 1848.

Answer: T

9. The Battle of Custoza represented a major setback for the Austrians.

Answer: F

10. Hungary might well have succeeded in gaining independence from Austria in 1849 had it not been for massive Russian military intervention to crush the uprising there.

Answer: T

Chronology

Place the following items in correct chronological order.

10. Louis Napoleon becomes emperor of the French
 8. Humiliation of Olmütz
 5. Battle of Custoza
 4. Frankfurt Parliament convenes
 7. Hungarian autonomy crushed by Russian invasion
 6. Louis Napoleon elected president of the new Second Republic
 1. Insurrection in Paris unseats Louis-Philippe
 2. Metternich flees to England
 9. Louis Napoleon's coup d'état
 3. June Days in Paris

Part Five
The Age of
Mass Politics

Chapter 18
The Era of
National Unification

This chapter relates the stirrings of nationalism in Italy, Germany, and the Habsburg lands, and the processes through which Italy and Germany were consolidated as unified nation-states.

Chapter Outline

I. Dreams of national independence

II. The political unification of Italy
 A. A long history of fragmentation
   1. Economic disparities
   2. Foreign domination
   3. The influence of the papacy
   4. Absence of centralized administration
   5. Disagreements over the form of a possible national government
 B. Leadership for Italian unification
   1. The nationalist sentiment of the "Risorgimento" (resurgence)
   2. One possibility: unification under the House of Savoy
   3. Cavour's innovative reforms
   4. A second possibility: Mazzini's nationalist republicanism
   5. "Young Italy" and the pressure of Mazzini's idealism
 C. Alliances and warfare
   1. Cavour plots to align Britain and France with Piedmont-Sardinia
   2. Cavour uses the Crimean War to further the aims of unification
   3. Mazzini's failed attempt to invade Naples (1857)
   4. Secret diplomacy at Plombières (1858)
   5. Austria clumsily walks into Cavour's trap (April 1859)
   6. Battles of Magenta and Solferino (June 1859)
   7. Louis Napoleon betrays Cavour and seeks compromise with Austria

        8.   Northern and central Italy come under Piedmontese rule (1860)

   D. Garibaldi and the liberation of southern Italy
       1.   Mazzinian background
       2.   The "red shirts" land in Sicily (1860)
       3.   End to papal and Bourbon rule in Italy

   E. Completion of Italy's unification
       1.   Austrians driven from Venetia (1866)
       2.   French forced to abandon Rome (1870)

   F. Political economy in unified Italy
       1.   Cavour's free trade policies hurt southern manufacturers
       2.   Growing disparities of wealth between north and south
       3.   A weak and inefficient political order

III. The unification of Germany
   A. Obstacles to unification
       1.   Upper classes wary of political change
       2.   Austrian or Prussian leadership?
       3.   Tensions between liberalism and nationalism

   B. Prussia's advantages

   C. Regional and ideological differences in the German states

   D. The constitutional crisis in Prussia
       1.   William I of Prussia accepts constitutional principles (1858)
       2.   The power of the Italian example in 1859
       3.   The National Union seeks a parliamentary government
       4.   Proposed reforms of the Prussian army
       5.   Stalemate between king and parliament over army reforms
       6.   Otto von Bismarck appointed Prussian chief minister (1862)
       7.   Bismarck's background and the ideology of Realpolitik
       8.   Bismarck proceeds with reforms despite parliament's opposition
       9.   Repression of liberal oppponents

   E. Alliances and warfare
       1.   Bismarck woos Russia (1863)
       2.   War over Schleswig-Holstein (1864)
       3.   Austro-Prussian War culminates in the Battle of Sadowa (1866)

   F. North German Confederation
       1.   Bismarck's moderation in dealing with defeated Austria
       2.   A new confederation, dominated by Prussia (1866)
       3.   Expansion of the Zollverein
       4.   Prussian liberals capitulate to Bismarck
       5.   Emergence of the National Liberal Party

    G. The Franco-Prussian war
1. Bismarck succeeds at isolating France diplomatically
2. French surrender, January 1871
3. Annexation of Alsace and Lorraine by Germany
4. Proclamation of German Empire (January 18, 1871)
5. An autocracy based on throne and aristocracy

IV. National awakenings in the Habsburg lands
    A. Linguistic, cultural, and historical diversity
1. Twenty nationalities
2. The potent idea of the monarchy itself as a unifying force
3. Vienna and German culture at the heart of the monarchy
4. Strong support from Austrian and Hungarian nobility
5. Catholicism as a force for unity
    B. Repression of nationalism
1. The "Patent" of 1851: a charter for neo-absolutism
2. Alexander von Bach uses state power to the fullest
    C. Political and military crises
1. The October Diploma (1860) dismantles the Bach system
2. The February Patent (1861)
3. Humiliating defeats of 1859 and 1866 cost the monarchy prestige
    D. Creation of the Dual Monarchy
1. A compromise between Vienna and the Magyars: the Ausgleich (1867)
2. Considerable administrative autonomy for Hungary
3. Dissatisfaction of non-Germans and non-Hungarians
    E. Precarious hold of a multinational empire in an age of nationalism

Suggestions for Lecture Topics

For a lecture on the nature of nationhood as a cultural creation, see the thought-provoking work by the anthropologist Benedict Anderson, *Imagined Communities*.

For nation-building in Italy, see Charles Delzell, ed., *The Unification of Italy*; and the biographies of Cavour, Garibaldi, and King Victor Emmanuel II by Denis Mack Smith.

For a pathbreaking recent study of German nationhood and its relation to religious sentiment, see Helmut Smith, *German Nationalism and Religious Conflict*.

For a pithy biography of Bismarck, full of excellent material for lectures, see A. J. P. Taylor, *Bismarck*.

For a gripping account of the secret diplomacy that preceded the unification of Italy, see Mack Walker, *Plombières*.

Multiple-Choice Questions

1. The word "Risorgimento" means
   a. rebirth.
   b. renaissance.
   c. unity.
   d. resurgence.
   e. none of the above

Answer: d

2. Which of the following was NOT an obstacle to Italian unification?
   a. economic disparities
   b. foreign domination
   c. the influence of the papacy
   d. disagreements over the form of a possible national government
   e. none of the above

Answer: e

3. Which of the following was the site of secret diplomacy between Cavour and Louis Napoleon leading toward the war against Austria of 1859?
   a. Plombières
   b. Magenta
   c. Solferino
   d. Sadowa
   e. Paris

Answer: a

4. Which of the following occurred in 1866?
   a. Austrians driven from Venetia
   b. Austrians defeated by Prussia
   c. Bismarck and Cavour meet secretly
   d. both a and c
   e. both a and b

Answer: e

5. After the Austro-Prussian War, Bismarck
   a. died.
   b. was promoted to prime minister.
   c. proclaimed the birth of a unified Germany.
   d. imposed a harsh punitive treaty on Austria.
   e. none of the above

Answer: e

6. The German Empire was officially created in
   a. 1859.
   b. 1866.
   c. 1870.
   d. 1871.
   e. none of the above

Answer: d

7. The word "*Realpolitik*" means
   a. realistic politics.
   b. actual policy.
   c. regal policy.
   d. ruthless politics.
   e. none of the above

Answer: a

8. The *Ausgleich* of 1867
   a. deeply humiliated King William I.
   b. created the Dual Monarchy.
   c. officially ended the Holy Roman Empire.
   d. officially ceded Bohemia to the Czechs.
   e. gave full autonomy to the Hungarians.

Answer: b

9. How many wars did Bismarck engage in between 1860 and 1871, in the process of bringing about the unification of Germany?
   a. one
   b. two
   c. three
   d. four
   e. five

Answer: c

10. The constitutional crisis of the 1860s in Prussia
    a.   was about parliamentary ratification of military funding.
    b.   pitted the liberals against the socialists.
    c.   pitted the king against the Junkers.
    d.   pitted Bismarck against the heir to the throne.
    e.   all of the above

Answer: a

Short-Answer Questions

1. Describe the difference between the aims of Mazzini, Garibaldi, and Cavour with regard to the future of Italy.
2. Describe the tension between liberalism and nationalism in Germany, and the role Bismarck played in mediating between the two.
3. What was significant about the Prussian constitutional crisis of the early 1860s? Why have historians tended to look back to this moment in German history as a particularly important one?
4. What were the major national, religious, or ethnic groups that made up the Habsburg monarchy? Why was nationalism inherently a threat to the survival of this monarchy? Explain.
5. Why did the Hungarians accept the *Ausgleich* of 1867? Why did they not push for full and complete independence? Explain.

True/False Questions

1. Bismarck was a Junker.

Answer: T

2. Cavour's first language was not Italian, but French.

Answer: T

3. Garibaldi hoped to become king of southern Italy.

Answer: F

4. Bismarck and Cavour worked closely together to further their nationalist aims.

Answer: F

5. Italy ceded Nice and Sardinia to France in 1859.

Answer: F

6. Austria and Prussia were allies in the war against Denmark of 1864.

Answer: T

7. German culture predominated in the Habsburg monarchy.

Answer: T

8. The words "Magyar" and "Hungarian" refer to the same people.

Answer: T

9. The words, "Slovenian," "Slovakian," and "Slavonian" refer to the same people.

Answer: F

10. The idea of the monarchy was itself a potent unifying force underlying the power of the Habsburg regime.

Answer: T

Chronology

Place the following items in the correct chronological order.

    8. *Ausgleich*

    9. Franco-Prussian War

    4. October Diploma

    3. Battle of Magenta

    7. Austrians driven from Venetia

    6. War over Schleswig-Holstein

    5. Bismarck appointed prime minister in Prussia

  10. Proclamation of German Empire

    2. Secret diplomacy at Plombières

    1. Crimean War

Chapter 19

The Dominant Powers in the Age of Liberalism: Britain, France, and Russia

This chapter describes the political and cultural developments that marked the mid-nineteenth century in Britain, Russia, and France. It focuses particularly on the movements for social and political reform that took place in each of these nations.

Chapter Outline

I.   Contrasting conditions in three European Great Powers

II. Victorian Britain
  A. Queen Victoria and Prince Albert
  B. Albert and the Great Exposition of 1851
    1. Symbol of a successful political and economic system
    2. Free trade and Britain's primacy in manufacturing
  C. Victorian notions of "respectability"
  D. The Victorian consensus
    1. The capitalist entrepreneurial ethic
    2. Darwin's theory of evolution (1859)
    3. Samuel Smiles and the doctrine of self-help
    4. Religious support for the Victorian consensus
    5. Moralizing the lower classes
  E. The Crimean War (1853–1856)
    1. Russian pressures on the declining Ottoman Empire
    2. British and Austrian resistance to Russian ambitions
    3. French ambitions
    4. A wretched war along the Black Sea
    5. Florence Nightingale launches nursing as a profession

      6. The Treaty of Paris (1856): humiliation for Russia
- F. The Liberal era
  1. Two decades of Whig rule (1850s and 1860s)
  2. Palmerston and chauvinism
  3. Gladstone and the Liberal Party
  4. Disraeli leads the Conservatives
- G. Working-class quiescence
  1. Trust in political reform
  2. The modest aims of workers' organizations
- H. The Reform Bill of 1867
  1. Questions over extending the suffrage
  2. A doubling of the number of men enfranchised
- I. The reforming state
  1. Chadwick's report on the living conditions of the poor (1842)
  2. Experts, statistics, and regulatory agencies
  3. The ideology of the "age of improvement"
  4. A broadening panoply of social services
  5. A professional civil service
  6. Regulation of working conditions
  7. The Education Act (1870)
  8. A flurry of state-sponsored reforms
- J. Conservative revival
  1. Creating a party for mass politics
  2. Nationalism and Tory reforms
  3. An end to the old "country/city" cleavage

III. Tsarist Russia
- A. The stirrings of reform
  1. Ninety-five percent of the population rural and backward
  2. Nicholas I attempts to seal off Russia from Western influence
  3. The conscience-stricken intelligentsia
  4. Westernizers versus Slavophiles
  5. Chaadayev, Belinsky, and Herzen champion change
- B. The emancipation of the serfs (1861)
  1. Economic incentives for reform
  2. The shock of the Crimean defeat
  3. Serf rebellions
  4. A less intransigent tsar, Alexander II
  5. Reorganization around peasant communes
  6. Contrasts with American abolition of slavery

       7. An expanded administrative apparatus
       8. Continued use and abuse of arbitrary state power
  C. An expanding empire
       1. The Crimean humiliation
       2. The Treaty of San Stefano (1878)
       3. Conquest to the east and south
  D. Nihilists and populists
       1. The nihilist rejection of all dogma
       2. Chernyshevsky's *What Is to Be Done?* (1863)
       3. Bakunin and the anarchists: destroying the state
       4. Populists: romantic peasant collectivists
       5. Assassination of Alexander II (1881)

IV. France's Second Empire
  A. The authoritarian empire (1852–1859)
       1. Crushing political opposition
       2. Patronage and the name of Bonaparte
       3. Loyalty of peasants and clergy to the regime
       4. Republicanism and socialism among workers
  B. Economic growth
       1. Rapid state-led expansion
       2. The Crédit Mobilier and Crédit Foncier
       3. The Suez Canal (1869)
       4. Railways and agriculture
  C. The rebuilding of Paris
       1. Baron Haussmann cuts wide swaths across the city
       2. Military implications of the boulevards
       3. Concerns for public health
       4. Increasing geographic segregation by class
       5. Parks vastly increased
  D. Science and realism
       1. Pasteur and germ theory (1860s)
       2. Positivism: the march of progress
       3. Comte and the stages of history
       4. Baudelaire and the art of self-discovery
       5. Painters of the Barbizon school reject romantic idealism
       6. Courbet and Millet: a new realism in painting
       7. Zola's novels
       8. Dostoevsky's explorations in Russia
       9. Renan's frank *Life of Jesus*

  10. Flaubert's rejection of bourgeois life
 E. Impressionism
  1. Choosing modern life as a subject
  2. Capturing the fleeting visual sensations of nature's scenes
  3. Official rejection of this innovative group's work
  4. Manet's challenge to classicism
  5. Monet turns away from realism
  6. Degas explores urban life
 F. The "Liberal Empire" (1859–1870)
  1. The Cobden-Chevalier Treaty (1860) promotes free trade
  2. Liberalizing reforms
  3. A weak and vacillating foreign policy
  4. The execution of Maximilian in Mexico (1867)
  5. Monarchists, republicans, and socialists mobilize
  6. The Ems Dispatch (1870)
 G. The Franco-Prussian War (1870–1871)
  1. A swift debacle for the French
  2. Paris fights on
  3. Adolphe Thiers negotiates with Bismarck
  4. The harsh Treaty of Frankfurt (May 10, 1871)
 H. The Paris Commune
  1. Civil war: republicans and socialists versus reactionary troops
  2. The Communards' social reforms
  3. The "Bloody Week": 25,000 dead in Paris
  4. A glimpse of a proletarian revolution?

Suggestions for Lecture Topics

For a lecture on Victorian culture, see Peter Gay, *The Bourgeois Experience*.

On the Crimean War, see Paul Schroeder, *Austria, Great Britain, and the Crimean War.*

For a lecture on tsarist Russia see David Saunders, *Russia in the Age of Reaction and Reform.*

For an overview of the historiography of France's Second Empire, see Stuart Campbell, *The Second Empire Revisited*; see also John Merriman, *The Red City.*

Students will enjoy a lecture on the artistic currents of realism and impressionism in France. Coupling the works of Millet and Courbet with readings from Zola makes a gripping combination for a lecture on realism.

In discussing impressionism, it is fascinating to the students if one brings to bear some of the developments in optics and the physiology of sight that helped pave the way for the impressionist approach to painting. See Diane Kelder, *The French Impressionists and Their Century.*

Multiple-Choice Questions

1. In what year was Britain's second Reform Bill passed?
   a. 1838
   b. 1848
   c. 1855
   d. 1867
   e. 1881

Answer: d

2. The Crystal Palace was
   a. Tsar Alexander's residence in St. Petersburg.
   b. Louis Napoleon's attempt to outdo Versailles.
   c. the exhibition hall of the Great Exposition of 1851.
   d. the place Bismarck chose to proclaim the German Empire.
   e. none of the above

Answer: c

3. Disraeli was
   a. a Whig.
   b. a socialist.
   c. a Tory.
   d. a Liberal.
   e. none of the above

Answer: c

4. Which of the following were Russian "Westernizers"?
   a. Bakunin
   b. Chernyshevsky
   c. Dostoevsky
   d. Chaadayev, Belinsky, and Herzen
   e. Pushkin

Answer: d

5. The Treaty of San Stefano was between which two nations?
   a. Britain and Russia
   b. Turkey and Russia
   c. Austria and Turkey
   d. France and Russia
   e. Austria and Bulgaria

Answer: b

6. In what year was the Suez Canal opened?
   a. 1869
   b. 1849
   c. 1877
   d. 1839
   e. 1855

Answer: a

7. Tsar Alexander was assassinated by
   a. an anarchist.
   b. a socialist.
   c. a populist.
   d. a nihilist.
   e. none of the above

Answer: a

8. Which of the following was NOT an impressionist?
   a. Manet
   b. Monet
   c. Degas
   d. Courbet
   e. Pissarro

Answer: d

9. The Paris Commune was crushed by
   a. French troops loyal to Louis Napoleon.
   b. French troops loyal to Thiers.
   c. German troops loyal to Bismarck.
   d. German troops acting as mercenaries for the French government.
   e. French and German troops acting together.

Answer: b

10. The Cobden-Chevalier Treaty
    a. recognized the existing borders of Belgium.
    b. recognized the existing borders of France.
    c. created an alliance between France and Britain in case of German aggression.
    d. imposed tariffs in France and Britain on all goods imported from third countries.
    e. none of the above

Answer: e

Short-Answer Questions

1. What role did religion play in the "Victorian consensus"?
2. Apart from the Reform Bill of 1867, what other significant reforms marked this period of British history? What motivated these reforms?
3. What were the reasons for the emancipation of the serfs in Russia in 1861? What impact did this have on the welfare of the Russian peasants?
4. What was the position taken by the Russian Slavophiles in their arguments against the Westernizers? Do you think these arguments had any merit? Explain.
5. What factors led Napoleon III to initiate liberalization of the Second Empire after 1859? What were the main results of this liberalization process?

True/False Questions

1. Samuel Smiles rejected Darwinian ideas.

Answer: F

2. Gladstone was a prominent conservative.

Answer: F

3. Tsar Nicholas II liberated Russia's serfs in 1861.

Answer: F

4. Russia was the effective loser of the Crimean War.

Answer: T

5. Chernyshevsky wrote *What Is to Be Done?*

Answer: T

6. The dictatorship of Louis Napoleon was approved of by many French citizens.

Answer: T

7. The dictatorship of Louis Napoleon marked a period of economic stagnation for France.

Answer: F

8. Comte was one of the creators of germ theory.

Answer: F

9. The Ems Dispatch helped trigger the Franco-Prussian War.

Answer: T

10. The Paris Commune was characterized by fervent religious spirit.

Answer: F

Chronology

Place the following items in correct chronological order.

    7. Franco-Prussian War begins

    6. Second British Reform Bill

    9. "Bloody Week" in Paris

    3. Crimean War begins

    1. Chadwick's report on living conditions of the poor

    2. Great Exposition in England

    8. Education Act

    5. Cobden-Chevalier Treaty

    4. Darwin publishes *On the Origin of Species*

   10. Alexander II assassinated

Chapter 20
Rapid Industrialization and Its Challenges, 1870–1914

This chapter describes the social and economic upheaval of the Second Industrial Revolution in Europe, as well as the cultural responses that accompanied it.

Chapter Outline

I.   A period of rapid economic and social change

II. The Second Industrial Revolution
    A. New technology and new industries
        1. The Bessemer process for steel production
        2. Electricity and social change
    B. Travel and communications
        1. Automobiles
        2. A revolution in concepts of space and time
        3. New patterns of leisure
    C. Regional variation
        1. Germany seizes the lead
        2. German banks, universities, and state policy foster growth
        3. English anxieties and disadvantages
        4. Russia remains backward, despite rapid industrialization
        5. France: slow but steady
        6. The "dual economies" of large parts of Europe

III. A changing population
    A. Demographic boom
        1. A 50 percent increase in European population (1870–1914)
        2. Births far outpace deaths
        3. French anxieties about slow population growth
        4. Decline of traditional family patterns

    B. Teeming cities
- 1. Factory towns booming
- 2. The rural exodus
- 3. Population of nine European cities tops one million by 1900
- 4. London's premier role
- 5. Social ills of the urban world
- 6. The expansion of suburbs

    C. Migration and emigration
- 1. An emerging global labor force
- 2. The interpenetration of urban and rural worlds
- 3. Massive overseas migration to the United States

IV. Social changes

    A. Industrial workers
- 1. Enormous differences in skill, status, and quality of life
- 2. "De-skilling" and the emergence of class consciousness
- 3. New professions emerging
- 4. Women and factory work

    B. Industrialization and the working family
- 1. Middle-class moral reforms
- 2. The break-up of families

    C. Prostitution
- 1. The Contagious Diseases Act in Britain (1864)
- 2. Josephine Butler's campaign for women's rights

    D. Improving standards of living for the working classes

    E. Social mobility
- 1. The growing middle classes
- 2. Increasing employment of women

V. Mass culture

    A. Education
- 1. Rising literacy
- 2. The Ferry Laws in France (1879–1881)
- 3. Regional differences
- 4. Education's role in perpetuating social cleavages
- 5. Teaching: a new profession for women
- 6. The limited scope of higher education

    B. The decline of organized religion
- 1. Regional "de-christianization"
- 2. Religion and gender roles

    C. Leisure

      1. Paris sets the tone for new modes of entertainment
      2. Bicycles and their social impact
  D. Sports
      1. The growth of team sports
      2. Olympic Games, first held in Athens in 1896
      3. Links with nationalistic ideologies
  E. Consumerism
      1. The new department stores
VI. Responses to a rapidly changing world
  A. A cultural crisis of previously unparalleled dimensions
      1. Alcoholism and drugs
  B. Artists' responses to mass society
      1. Mass culture vs. high culture
      2. William Morris: decrying the uniformity of the machine age
      3. Monet, Pissarro, and the critics of modernity
  C. Scientists
      1. New knowledge brings new mysteries
      2. Physicists challenge contemporary notions of matter
      3. Einstein's General Principle of Relativity (1915)
  D. Social theorists
      1. Weber and the impersonal "age of bureaucracy"
      2. Durkheim and "alienation"
      3. Le Bon and the emergence of "crowd theory"
  E. Freud and the study of the irrational
      1. Family origins
      2. The development of psychoanalysis
      3. The power of the irrational
  F. Nietzsche
      1. Harsh critic of all religion
  G. The avant-garde
      1. Diaghilev's provocative ballets in Paris
      2. A rebellion against rationalism
      3. Outsiders and rebels
      4. Between patronage and the rejection of "respectability"
      5. New structures in musical composition
      6. Pointillism and post-impressionism
      7. Art nouveau and the influence of psychology
      8. Vienna as a capital of the avant-garde
      9. Picasso's modernism
      10. Cubism: the return to basic shapes in painting

11. The futurists' embrace of modernity

Suggestions for Lecture Topics

For a basic work on the industrialization process, see David Landes, *The Unbound Prometheus.*

For a lecture on the rise of mass culture, see Standish Meacham, *A Life Apart*, and Raymond Williams, *The Long Revolution.*

A reading from Zola's *Germinal* during part of a lecture can help to bridge the substantial gap between most American college students and the world of the European working class at the turn of the century.

Students tend to be fascinated by Nietzsche's challenge to religion and conventional morality. A brief lecture on some of the main points of his philosophy, followed by class discussion of such issues as moral relativism or of the role of religion in society, tend to elicit strong responses from many students who would otherwise shy away from participation. For an excellent recent work on this subject, see Charles Taylor, *Sources of the Self.*

For a lecture on Freud, see Philip Rieff, *Freud: The Mind of the Moralist.*

A spectacular study of the avant-garde, from which both slides and lecture material can be drawn, is Carl Schorske, *Fin de Siècle Vienna.*

Multiple-Choice Questions

1. The "department store" was first created in
    a. New York.
    b. Paris.
    c. London.
    d. Berlin.
    e. Vienna.

Answer: b

2. The Bessemer process caused a revolution in the production of what material?
    a. cotton
    b. iron
    c. electricity
    d. automobiles
    e. none of the above

Answer: e

3. The standard of living for the working classes during the late nineteenth century was
    a. declining slowly.
    b. rising slowly.
    c. declining rapidly.
    d. remaining even.
    e. none of the above

Answer: b

4. The Ferry Laws in France
    a. regulated child labor.
    b. regulated prostitution.
    c. established a universal educational system.
    d. established a universal health care system.
    e. both a and b

Answer: c

5. The first Olympic Games were held in 1896 in
    a. Athens.
    b. Olympia.
    c. Paris.
    d. London.
    e. Rome.

Answer: a

6. William Morris was
    a. a British socialist.
    b. a British artist.
    c. a Welsh poet.
    d. an Irish industrialist.
    e. both a and b

Answer: e

7. Einstein's *General Principle of Relativity* was first published in
    a. 1875.
    b. 1895.
    c. 1911.
    d. 1915.
    e. 1921.

Answer: d

8. Which of the following was a major theorist of crowd behavior?
   a. Weber
   b. Durkheim
   c. Le Bon
   d. Jarry
   e. Pissarro

Answer: c

9. Josephine Butler was
   a. an artist.
   b. a social reformer.
   c. a musician.
   d. a dancer.
   e. an actress.

Answer: b

10. Which of the following was one of the major capitals of the avant-garde?
   a. Rome
   b. Madrid
   c. London
   d. Stuttgart
   e. Vienna

Answer: e

Short-Answer Questions

1. What were the principal new technologies of the Second Industrial Revolution, and what was their impact on society? In what ways were some (or perhaps all) aspects of this social impact unintended and/or unforeseeable? Explain.
2. Describe what is meant by the term "dual economy" in the description of economic conditions during many parts of Europe during the late nineteenth century.
3. Describe what is meant by the term "de-skilling" and explain its impact on those whom it affected.
4. What is meant by the term "mass culture"? Describe some of the principal forms of mass culture that emerged during the period covered by this chapter.

5. Why is the cultural response to the newly emerging industrial order referred to as a "cultural crisis?" What was the crisis about? What were some of the "traditional" cultural norms that were being rejected by many European artists and thinkers during the late nineteenth century, and what were their reasons for doing so?

True/False Questions

1. Bessemer was an expert on mass production techniques.

Answer: F

2. Two of the most important technological factors in the Second Industrial Revolution were steel and electricity.

Answer: T

3. Between 1870 and 1914, Europe's population increased by 50 percent.

Answer: T

4. With the advance of female employment in the factories, the number of prostitutes in most European cities gradually declined during the nineteenth century.

Answer: F

5. The Contagious Diseases Act did not render prostitution illegal.

Answer: T

6. The Olympic Games were created by a Frenchman.

Answer: T

7. Max Weber invented a revolutionary new form of automobile tire.

Answer: F

8. Contrary to popular belief, the words "God is dead" do not appear in any of Nietzsche's writings.

Answer: F

9. Einstein believed that the speed of light was relative, because it changed depending on where in the universe the light was coming from.

Answer: F

10. The futurists were extremely pessimistic about the impact of technology on humanity's long-term prospects.

Answer: F

Chronology

Place the following items in correct chronological order.

   10. Einstein's *General Principle of Relativity*
    5. Ferry laws in France
    1. Contagious Diseases Act in Britain
    7. First Olympic Games held
    4. Edison invents incandescent lamp
    3. Bell invents telephone
    6. Radioactivity discovered
    2. Stock market crash fuels depression in nineteenth-century Europe
    9. *Rite of Spring* first plays before an audience in Paris
    8. Picasso paints *Les Demoiselles D'Avignon*

Chapter 21
Mass Politics and Nationalism

This chapter analyzes the rising force of nationalist ideology as it emerged in different forms and in different contexts in each of the major European powers. The chapter also scrutinizes the new political forms that channeled the growing involvement of the European masses in the governance of their countries.

Chapter Outline

I.   Mass politics on the left and right
    A.   Growth of the state
    B.   Secularization

II. From liberalism to nationalism
    A.   A new national political life
        1.   Mass parties
        2.   Widening suffrage
        3.   Mass literacy
        4.   Popular press
    B.   The waning of the liberal era
        1.   Challenges from both left and right
    C.   Universal male suffrage
        1.   France (1871)
        2.   Germany (1880)
        3.   Britain (1884, with property restrictions)
        4.   Austria (1907)
        5.   Italy (1912)
    D.   The "long depression" of 1873–1896
        1.   A Viennese financial crash spreads rapidly throughout Europe
    E.   Economic cartels
        1.   Debates over tariffs rage even in England

  F. The new nationalism
    1. Anti-democratic in nature
    2. Anti-Semitism
    3. Imperialism
    4. New associations, leagues, and mass publications
    5. Conservatives stirred to fear by the rising power of the left
    6. The appeal to the pivotal lower middle class

III. Social reform
  A. Burgeoning trade unions
    1. Strikes and demonstrations increase dramatically
    2. Workers resent new modes of factory discipline
    3. "Taylorism" and scientific management
    4. Limits to union membership
    5. Women and trade unions
  B. State social reform
    1. Imperial Germany leads the way under Bismarck
    2. British Labour Party (1901) adds to reformist consensus
    3. Modest reforms in France
  C. Women's suffrage
    1. Severe restrictions on women's rights well into 1900s
    2. Men on left, center, and right agree on subjection of women
    3. Feminism emerges during late nineteenth century
    4. Militant suffragettes in Britain

IV. Challengers to the nation–state
  A. The Catholic Church
    1. An alternative focus of allegiance
    2. The Papal *Syllabus of Errors* of 1864
    3. Church support for authoritarian regimes
    4. Leo XIII, *Rerum Novarum*, and Christian Socialists
  B. Socialists
    1. A ubiquitous social and political force
    2. Internationalism as ideology
    3. Reformists versus revolutionaries
    4. The Erfurt Congress of 1891
    5. Guesde's Socialist Workers' Party in France (1883)
    6. Revolutionary "Westernizers" in Russia
    7. British Fabians
    8. The German SPD: 35 percent of the vote by 1912
    9. Millerand and Jaurès in France

    C. Anarchism
1. Kropotkin's vision of a stateless society
2. Spain and Italy: anarchist strongholds
3. A wave of assassinations and bombings
    D. Syndicalism
1. Free associations of producers to replace the state
2. Sorel's *Reflections on Violence* (1908)
3. Labor exchanges
4. State repression

V. Changes and continuities in British political life
  A. Liberal reforms continue under Chamberlain
  B. Irish home rule
1. Gladstone's moral crusade on behalf of Irish rights
2. Parnell's moderate program of reform
3. Captain Boycott and the "land war" (1879–1882)
4. British repression
5. Liberal Party divided over home rule
  C. New contours in British political life
1. Conservative rule, 1895–1905
2. Trade union militancy after 1880
3. The successful dock workers' strike of 1889
4. Anti-union Taff Vale decision in the House of Lords (1901)
5. Birth of the Labour Party (1901)
6. Splits on the right after 1905
7. Trades Disputes Act (1906) reverses Taff Vale
8. Lloyd George leads the Liberals against the House of Lords
9. The Parliament Act (1911) limits power of House of Lords
10. Reformers among the working class
11. Irish home rule festers on the eve of war in 1914

VI. Republican France
  A. Monarchists and republicans
1. Count of Chambord vs. Count of Paris
2. Catholic support of monarchism
3. France in 1873: republic with monarchist institutions
4. Constitutional ambiguities
5. MacMahon's political crisis of May 16, 1877
  B. The Third Republic
1. "Opportunists" at the center of the political spectrum
2. The Boulanger Affair and the "new right" (1889)

3.   Catholic support for the republic grows
4.   Édouard Drumont and the Panama Canal scandal (1889)
C.   The Dreyfus Affair
1.   Right against left
2.   Army, Church, and monarchists vs. republicans and socialists
3.   Arrest (1894) and conviction of Dreyfus
4.   Rampant anti-Semitism in France
5.   A high-level cover-up
6.   Zola to the rescue: "J'accuse!"
7.   Charles Maurras and Action Française
8.   Full exoneration of Dreyfus in 1906
D.   The Radical Republic
1.   Separation of church and state
2.   Clemenceau and Poincaré: aggressive nationalism

VII. Tsarist Russia
A.   Russification
1.   Russian language imposed in schools
2.   Russian Orthodox Church imposed against non-Orthodox religions
B.   The Russo-Japanese War (1904-1905)
1.   Conflict of interests in Asia
2.   The Battle of Mukden (March 1905)
3.   The Battle of Tsushima (May 1905)

VIII. Italy
A.   Resistance to the state
1.   Intense regional and local loyalties
2.   Suspicion of national unity in the south
3.   North-south economic disparity
4.   Continued implacable opposition from the Church
B.   Centralized authority
1.   *Trasformismo*: a maelstrom of shifting political coalitions
2.   Crispi's authoritarian methods
3.   Alliance between northern industrialists, southern landowners
4.   The age of Giolitti
5.   Growth of the anti-parliamentary right
6.   Giolitti's alliance with the Church
C.   The rise of Italian nationalism
1.   Defeat of Italian troops at Adowa (1896)
2.   Invasion and conquest of Libya (1911)

IX. Austria-Hungary
  A. Ethnic tensions
     1. Hungarian resentment of Germanic dominance
     2. Everyone else's resentment of Hungarian and Germanic dominance
  B. Forces of cohesion
     1. The personal prestige of the emperor
     2. Catholic and army support
  C. Nationalist movements
     1. Polish and Serb nationalism
     2. Magyarization vs. Pan-Slavism

X. Germany
  A. Nationalist vs. internationalist movements
     1. Bismarck's hatred for both Catholics and socialists
     2. The *Kulturkampf* (1873)
     3. Antisocialist legislation (1878)
  B. William II and nationalism
     1. William II's accession to the throne (1888)
     2. Bismarck resigns (1890)
     3. Aggressive and provocatory foreign policy
     4. Conservatives, National Liberals, and Catholic Center Party
     5. Even socialists espouse nationalist ideology

Suggestions for Lecture Topics

A superb source for a lecture on the waning years of liberalism is George Dangerfield's *The Strange Death of Liberal England*.

The Dreyfus Affair makes a fascinating subject for a lecture, perhaps followed by opening up the pro-Dreyfus and anti-Dreyfus positions for debate by the class. For background sources, see Albert Lindemann, *The Jew Accused*.

The experience of the suffragettes, particularly in England, also makes an absorbing lecture topic. See Sandra Holton, *Feminism and Democracy*.

Anti-Semitism—particularly the reasons why it was strong in some nations and weaker in others—tends to fascinate students. A major theoretical work on the roots of this phenomenon is Hannah Arendt, *The Origins of Totalitarianism*.

The intricacies and nuances of the European left will require extensive clarification for American students, who tend to see the left in rather stark and monolithic terms. For a superb overview of the various strands on the left, see Leszek Kolakowski, *Main Currents of Marxism*.

Multiple-Choice Questions

1. General MacMahon was
   a.   a British officer accused of treason.
   b.   a British officer who blocked an assassination attempt on the king.
   c.   a British officer who opposed Irish home rule.
   d.   both b and c
   e.   none of the above

Answer: e

2. Which of the following was a major theorist of anarchism?
   a.   Sorel
   b.   Guesde
   c.   Jaurès
   d.   Kropotkin
   e.   Millerrand

Answer: d

3. Taff Vale was
   a.   a British admiral.
   b.   a landmark decision by the House of Lords.
   c.   an Irish nationalist.
   d.   the place where Gladstone was assassinated.
   e.   none of the above

Answer: b

4. The word "boycott" comes from
   a.   an Irish nationalist leader.
   b.   a British feminist leader.
   c.   a Russian word for "avoid."
   d.   a French word for "punish."
   e.   none of the above

Answer: a

5. *Rerum Novarum* was
   a.   a papal encyclical opposing many aspects of modernity.
   b.   a papal encyclical accepting many aspects of modernity.
   c.   a French newspaper espousing anti-Semitism.
   d.   a French newspaper opposing anti-Semitism.
   e.   a novel by Zola.

Answer: b

6. "J'accuse!" was written by
   a.   Clemenceau
   b.   Drumont
   c.   Boulanger
   d.   Zola
   e.   Dreyfus

Answer: d

7. The Battle of Tsushima was
   a.   a victory for the Russians.
   b.   a crushing defeat for the Russians.
   c.   a skirmish leading to the Battle of Mukden.
   d.   the first defeat of a European power by a non-European power.
   e.   none of the above

Answer: b

8. The word "trasformismo" refers to
   a.   an electrical appliance invented in Italy in 1882.
   b.   an electrical appliance invented in Italy in 1907.
   c.   a political process of shifting coalitions in Italy.
   d.   an attempt by the Mafia to shift attention away from itself.
   e.   an attempt by Italian politicians to shift blame for poverty to the Mafia.

Answer: c

9. The two dominant ethnic groups in the Habsburg monarchy were
   a.   Austrians and Magyars
   b.   Czechs and Croats
   c.   Serbs and Austrians
   d.   Hungarians and Bohemians
   e.   Germans and Slavs

Answer: a

10. The *Kulturkampf* was
  a.   a book written by Goethe.
  b.   Bismarck's campaign against socialists.
  c.   Bismarck's campaign for educational reform.
  d.   Bismarck's campaign against liberals.
  e.   Bismarck's campaign against Catholics.

Answer: e

Short-Answer Questions

1. What were the main forces behind the "new nationalism" that emerged in Europe in the last three decades of the nineteenth century? What was "new" about this nationalism? Explain.
2. What were the major groups within the European left at the turn of the century, and what ideological and practical points defined the differences among them?
3. A famous book about England in the first decade of the 1900s is entitled, *The Strange Death of Liberal England*. What did the author mean by the "death" of a "liberal" England? What was the "liberal" order, and what forces were pushing it aside at the turn of the century?
4. What was at stake in the Dreyfus Affair? Describe both the immediate issues and the deeper social and political issues involved.
5. Some historians have described the advent to power of William II in Germany, and the departure of Bismarck from the scene, as a catastrophe for Europe. Do you agree? Explain. What had Bismarck succeeded at doing while in power, and what happened after he was no longer in power?

True/False Questions

1. The British Labour Party was created in 1901.

Answer: T

2. Sorel wrote *Reflections on Violence*.

Answer: T

3. "Taylorism" refers to strike-breaking activity.

Answer: F

4. Universal male suffrage was introduced in Germany in 1880.

Answer: T

5. From 1873 to about 1896, Europe was stricken by an economic depression.

Answer: T

6. The Fabians were revolutionary leftists.

Answer: F

7. Anti-Semitism was widespread in late-nineteenth-century France.

Answer: T

8. Giolitti was a famous Italian anarchist.

Answer: F

9. Russia lost the war with Japan of 1904–1905.

Answer: T

10. Italy lost the war with Ethiopia of 1896.

Answer: T

Chronology

Place the following items in correct chronological order.

    2. Beginning of French Third Republic
    7. British Labour Party formed
    9. Taff Vale decision overturned
    1. Papal *Syllabus of Errors*
    5. Dreyfus arrested
    8. Battle of Tsushima
    6. Battle of Adowa
    3. *Kulturkampf* in Germany
    10. Dreyfus exonerated
    4. Bismarck steps down as chancellor

Chapter 22

The Age of European Imperialism

This chapter provides an overview of European imperialism from approximately 1870 to the First World War, exploring the underlying causes as well as the avowed motivations for this rapid expansion of European power. The nature of imperial domination is described, and the consequences for both the Great Powers and their subject territories are set forth.

Chapter Outline

I. A paradigmatic case: The Belgian Congo
   A. The Congress of Berlin, 1884–1885
   B. Brutal excesses under King Leopold

II. Definitions of imperialism
   A. Military control
   B. Economic and strategic interests
   C. Differentiation from colonialism
      1. Colonialism: direct settlement from the metropolitan power
      2. Imperialism: fewer settlers, more indirect control
   D. Pre-nineteenth-century forerunners
   E. Holdings of the major European powers by the mid-nineteenth century

III. The scramble for Africa (1870s to 1890s)
   A. Intra-European nationalist rivalries
   B. Britain vs. France
      1. Psychological impact of the Franco-Prussian War
      2. French visions of economic expansion in Africa
      3. Conflicts over the Suez Canal and Egypt
      4. Rivalry in Central Africa
   C. Germany enters the race

        1.   Pressures on Bismarck from the German colonial lobby
        2.   German holdings in Africa
   D. Italy's colonial misadventures
   E. The Fashoda Affair (1898)
   F. The Boer War (1899–1902)
        1.   British colonialists vs. indigenous Zulus and Dutch colonists
        2.   The discovery of diamonds and its impact
        3.   The role of a tenacious individual, Cecil Rhodes
        4.   The Jameson raid (1895)
        5.   A war unpopular for Britain both at home and abroad
        6.   The armistice of 1902 and its legacy

IV. Imperialism in Asia
   A. India
        1.   The British East India Company
        2.   Opium and British trade with the Orient
        3.   The Sepoy Mutiny (1857)
        4.   Lord Curzon, Queen Victoria, and the beginning of direct rule
        5.   British reforms and economic development in India
   B. Southeast Asia
        1.   Dutch domination over Indonesia
        2.   French Indochina
        3.   South Pacific island holdings
   C. Japan's unique status
        1.   The Meiji Restoration and its westernizing consequences
        2.   Economic and technological expansion
   D. China in decline
        1.   Forced concessions to Japan, Germany, Russia, and France
        2.   The U.S. responds with the "open door" concept
        3.   The Boxer Rebellion (1900)
        4.   The Russo-Japanese War (1904–1905)
   E. The United States as an imperial power
        1.   Conquest of the Philippines

V. The harsh realities of imperialism
   A. Assumptions of European superiority
   B. Social Darwinism
        1.   Herbert Spencer applies the theory of evolution to entire peoples
        2.   Cultural stereotypes
        3.   Attempted extermination of the Herero in German Southwest Africa

       4.   "Social imperialism": defusing social tensions within the European powers

  C. European technological advantages vs. indigenous resistance

  D. Economic aspects of imperialism
1. Expropriation and forced labor
2. Free trade vs. monopoly practices
3. Taxation as a vehicle of exploitation

  E. Administrative methods
1. "Formal" vs. "informal" imperialism: a question of degree
2. Shifting meanings of the term "protectorate"
3. The case of the Ashanti kingdom: inexorably deepening involvement
4. Independent trading companies committed European governments to increasingly direct rule
5. The British policy of "divide and rule"
6. French centralization and reliance on fewer indigenous intermediaries than the British

VI. Goals and motivations of imperialism
  A. The "civilizing mission"
1. Spreading Christianity
2. Abolishing slavery and curbing indentured servitude
3. The "dual mandate" as a justification for domination

  B. Economic factors assessed
1. Raw materials and new markets
2. J. A. Hobson: empire as an outlet for capital and products
3. Lenin: competition for empire as the root of war
4. The economic depression of 1873–1896 as a causal factor
5. Economic benefits to the colonial powers
6. The small percentage of capital invested in empire
7. Economic costs to the colonial powers
8. The lure of future riches

  C. Nationalism and Great-Power rivalries
1. The case of Britain and Burma: keeping the French out

  D. The quest for adventure and the exotic

  E. Critics of imperialism: moral and economic arguments

  F. Conclusion

Suggestions for Lecture Topics

For a lecture on the experience of being a colonial administrator, see the extraordinarily candid account given by George Orwell in his short essay, "Shooting an Elephant." An excellent companion reading to this essay is the short story by Doris Lessing, "The Old Chief Mshlanga," in which she describes growing up in South Africa under the apartheid system. Both these readings would also work very well as foci for short essay assignments for undergraduates.

The background for a lecture on the economic aspects of imperialism is ably presented in Bernard Porter, *The Lion's Share*.

For a lecture on the critics of imperialism, see Bernard Semmel, *Imperialism and Social Reform*, and A. P. Thornton, *The Imperial Idea and Its Enemies*.

A lecture on Gandhi—perhaps with an evening showing of the film by that title—would raise all the key issues involved in imperialism, while providing the compellingly clear focus of a biographical narrative. Gandhi's autobiography provides useful background material for an introductory lecture on the topic.

For a lecture on the ideological aspects of imperialism, particularly European assumptions of superiority, see Edward Said, *Orientalism*.

For a lecture focusing on the distinction between "formal" vs. "informal" imperialism, see the book by Gallagher and Robinson, *Africa and the Victorians*.

Films that deal directly with the topic of imperialism make excellent material to supplement lectures: *Sugar Cane Alley* (about French Martinique); *Gandhi* and *A Passage to India* (about India); *Heart of Darkness* (about the Congo); *Indochine* (about French Indochina); *The Last Emperor* (Bernardo Bertolucci's evocation of the declining Chinese court); *Out of Africa* (on Kenya). All these films work very well as jumping-off points for class discussion.

Multiple-Choice Questions

1. King Leopold of Belgium
   a. was forced to give up his colonial holdings under British pressure.
   b. presided personally over the creation of a vast colony in the Congo.
   c. became famous for his kind treatment of colonized Africans.
   d. gave up his crown to become a colonial explorer.
   e. is correctly represented by all the above statements.

Answer: b

2. Imperialism is different from colonialism because
   a. imperialism represents military conquest whereas colonialism results from purely economic domination.
   b. imperialism was carried out for religious reasons, whereas colonialism was carried out for political reasons.
   c. colonialism was characterized by high levels of direct settlement by Europeans, whereas imperialism was not.
   d. colonialism happened only before the nineteenth century, and no longer existed after the year 1848.
   e. both a and d

Answer: c

3. The "new imperialism" of the late-nineteenth century
   a. was caused by nationalist rivalries among European powers.
   b. was caused by the search for raw materials and new markets.
   c. almost brought France and Britain to war with each other.
   d. was seen by Lenin as a cause of the First World War.
   e. is correctly represented by all the above statements.

Answer: e

4. The only major Asian country to escape European domination in the late-nineteenth century was
   a. Japan.
   b. China.
   c. Vietnam.
   d. Formosa.
   e. Manchuria.

Answer: a

5. The Boer War
   a. was fought by the British to aid Dutch settlers against the Zulus.
   b. was the only war lost by Britain in the nineteenth century.
   c. brought Britain a high degree of diplomatic isolation.
   d. was the first war in which the British introduced the Maxim gun.
   e. was fought by Britain to aid the Italians in their colonial pursuits.

Answer: c

6. The German Chancellor Otto von Bismarck
   a. was enthusiastic about imperialism from the start.
   b. was an opponent of imperialism, but reluctantly agreed to it.

    c.   was in favor of colonialism, but not in favor of imperialism.

    d.   feared that an empire in Africa would bankrupt the German treasury.

    e.   remained opposed to imperialism all his life.

Answer: b

7. The Chinese empire was dominated by
    a. Germany and Britain and France.
    b. France and the U.S. and Russia.
    c. Japan and Russia and Britain.
    d. Japan and France and Britain.
    e. all of the above nations

Answer: e

8. Most European empires
    a. made a profit for their colonizing nations.
    b. ended up costing more than they yielded in revenues for their colonizing nations.
    c. became important markets for European manufactured goods.
    d. traded with each other more than they did with European nations.
    e. both c and d

Answer: b

9. Social Darwinism
    a. is a theory about racial differences among the world's peoples.
    b. holds that "survival of the fittest" applies to human beings as well as animals.
    c. is a theory named after the man who created it, Charles Darwin.
    d. Both a and b, but not c are true.
    e. Both b and c, but not a are true.

Answer: d

10. The Sepoy Mutiny took place because
    a. Hindus and Muslims resented the policy of using animal fat to lubricate ammunition cartridges.
    b. Hindus felt that Muslims had gotten special treatment by the British.
    c. Muslims felt that Hindus had gotten special treatment by the British.
    d. the Sepoys, a religious organization, wanted to create a Buddhist government.

e.   the Sepoys, a religious organization, wanted to create a Christian government.

Answer: a

Short-Answer Questions

1. What kinds of factors led the Europeans to treat the subjects of imperialism harshly and sometimes brutally?
2. What kinds of factors led to the "Scramble for Africa" of the late nineteenth century?
3. Why did Japan succeed at fending off European domination, whereas China did not?
4. What do we mean by "Social Darwinism"? How is it different from the Darwinian theory of evolution?
5. On balance, do you think that economic factors were more important in shaping imperialism—or were the moral factors (the "civilizing mission") more important? Discuss.

True/False Questions

1. The Boxer Rebellion took place in India.

Answer: F

2. The Fashoda Affair caused the Russo-Japanese War of 1904–1905.

Answer: F

3. Cecil Rhodes was a prominent British supporter of imperialism.

Answer: T

4. The statesman Ramsey MacDonald was a prominent British supporter of imperialism.

Answer: F

5. The Franco-Prussian War helped cause France to turn toward imperial expansion.

Answer: T

6. The Suez Canal was dug by the French.

Answer: T

7. The Suez Canal made huge profits for the British.

Answer: T

8. The economic depression of 1873–1896 acted as a brake upon the "Scramble for Africa."

Answer: F

9. Christian missionaries successfully agitated to secure better treatment for indigenous peoples in most European colonies.

Answer: F

10. Privately owned, independent trading companies allowed European governments to get steadily less involved in their colonies.

Answer: F

Chronology

Place the following items in correct chronological order.
4. Congress of Berlin
6. Fashoda Affair
7. Boer War
8. Boxer Rebellion
2. Sepoy Mutiny
9. Russo-Japanese War
10. World War I
3. Finishing of the Suez Canal
5. Battle of Adowa
1. British colonize India

Chapter 23
The Origins of the Great War

This chapter details both the short-term and the longer-term causes of World War I, ranging from military and geopolitical factors, such as the Great Powers' imperial rivalries and the alliance system, to cultural and social factors, such as nationalism and Social Darwinist theories of war.

Chapter Outline

I.   Visions of war in 1914
    A.   The rare few who anticipated unprecedented bloodshed
    B.   The overconfident many

II. The formation of the Triple Alliance among Germany, Austria-Hungary, and Italy (1880)
    A.   Tensions between France and Germany
        1.   The legacy of the Franco-Prussian War of 1870–1871
        2.   Colonial rivalries
    B.   Centrifugal forces within the Habsburg Monarchy
        1.   Czechs, Slovaks, and Romanians
        2.   South Slavs chafe at Austro-Hungarian domination
        3.   Russian Pan-Slav support for rebellious Serbs
    C.   Russian designs on the Ottoman Empire
    D.   The Dual Alliance of 1879 between Germany and Austria-Hungary
    E.   The Dual Alliance becomes Triple: Italy joins in 1880

III. The emergence of the Triple Entente among France, Britain, and Russia (1907)
    A.   The internal logic of the alliance system
        1.   Instability of alignments among five Great Powers
        2.   Great-Power hegemony over lesser powers
        3.   Secret treaties
    B.   A rift comes to divide Russia from Germany and Austria-Hungary

   1. The Three Emperors' League of 1873
   2. The divisive issue of the Balkans
  C. Russia and France overcome their differences and forge an alliance
   1. Cultural commonalities
   2. French economic investment in Russian industrialization
   3. A defensive alliance is signed in 1894
   4. Bismarck's nightmare comes true: Germany faces a war on two fronts
  D. The emergence of the Anglo–German rivalry
   1. Britain emerges from its "splendid isolation"
   2. The unpopular Boer War and German reactions to it
   3. Economic competition
   4. The naval rivalry caused by Germany's expansion of its fleet; the role played by the German admiral Alfred von Tirpitz
   5. The Pan-German League
   6. Britain counters with the formidable Dreadnought class warship
  E. Britain and France build the Entente Cordiale (1904)
   1. Settling old disputes between the two democracies
   2. The First Moroccan Crisis: the Entente put to the test
   3. The Algeciras Conference of 1906
   4. Britain mends fences with France's ally, Russia
  F. Russia, Britain, and France form the Triple Entente (1907)

IV. Europe divided into two hostile camps
  A. Germany forced into unconditional support of Austria-Hungary
  B. Balkan nationalisms
   1. Serbia and Austria-Hungary increasingly at odds
   2. Instability of the Ottoman Empire and Russian designs on it
  C. The Bosnian Crisis of 1908
   1. Austria-Hungary annexes Bosnia and Herzegovina
   2. Serbia and Russia forced to accept a *fait accompli*
   3. The fissures between the armed camps become wider
  D. The Second Moroccan Crisis (1911)
   1. France turns Morocco into a full-fledged protectorate
   2. Germany demands compensation from France's colonies
  E. The Balkan Wars
   1. The First Balkan War: Serbia, Bulgaria, Montenegro, and Greece defeat Turkey (1912)
   2. The Second Balkan War: expansionist Bulgaria is defeated by Serbia and Greece (1913)

V. An overview of causal factors
    A. Military planners considered war inevitable and even desirable
        1. Pressures for early mobilization
        2. Social Darwinist beliefs: war as "natural"
    B. Domestic politics and the possibility of war
        1. Nationalism in all the Great Powers
        2. Popular images of the enemy in Britain
        3. French desires to regain Alsace-Lorraine
        4. Russian ambivalence
        5. German aggressive patriotism
    C. Imperial rivalries
    D. Personal characteristics of Europe's leaders

VI. The final spark that set off the powder keg
    A. The assassination of Austro-Hungarian archduke Francis Ferdinand
        in Sarajevo, capital of Bosnia (June 28, 1914)
    B. Austria-Hungary's hard-line response against the Serbs
        1. The German "blank check"
    C. The Austro-Hungarian ultimatum to Serbia
    D. Flurry of diplomatic activity in the capitals of Europe
    E. Russian mobilization (July 25)
    F. Germany and the Schlieffen Plan
        1. How to fight and win a two-front war
        2. Phase I: knock France out quickly in a lightning attack passing
            through Belgium
        3. Phase II: after defeating France, turn to the east and face the
            more slowly mobilizing Russians
    G. Serbia responds to the Austro-Hungarian ultimatum; Austria-Hungary
        declares war on Serbia
    H. War fever spreads among all the parties
    I. Vain last-ditch efforts to forestall the conflict
    J. August 3, 1914: Germany attacks France through Belgium, whose
        neutrality was guaranteed by Britain
    K. Britain declares war on Germany (August 4)

Suggestions for Lecture Topics

For a lecture on the causes of the war, see the book by Laurence Lafore,
The Long Fuse. This book is sufficiently clear in its examination of the various
factors to make excellent supplemental reading for undergraduates.

The subject of German expansionism, both before and during the war, would make an excellent lecture topic. See Fritz Fischer, *Germany's Aims in the First World War* and John Maynard Keynes, *The Economic Consequences of the Peace*, for two conflicting appraisals of Germany's status as an aggressor nation.

In order to keep students from becoming hopelessly confused by the tangled issues of pre-war Balkan politics, it would be a good idea to devote an entire lecture to this topic—particularly since many aspects of these nationalistic and ethnic tensions have resurfaced tragically in the wake of the ending of the Cold War. These issues have hence acquired a certain direct contemporary relevance.

One possibility for an excellent class debate would be to compare the alliance system preceding World War I, with its two rival blocs, to the East-West rivalry that characterized the Cold War geopolitics of the post-1945 era. Ferreting out the various similarities and differences makes a most instructive exercise.

V. I. Lenin's book, *Imperialism: the Highest Stage of Capitalism*, gives an intriguing interpretation of the war's causes. A lecture on this topic, perhaps with an accompanying class discussion, would help to illuminate not only the strengths and weaknesses of Lenin's position itself, but would also give students a good opportunity to clarify in their own minds the various causal factors and how they need to be sorted out and understood in relation to each other.

Multiple-Choice Questions

1. Which nations formed the Triple Alliance?
   a. Italy, Russia, and Austria-Hungary
   b. Britain, France, and Russia
   c. Germany, Austria-Hungary, and Italy
   d. Britain, Belgium, and Serbia
   e. none of the above

Answer: c

2. Which nations formed the Triple Entente?
   a. France, Britain, and Italy
   b. France, Russia, and Italy
   c. France, Belgium, and Britain
   d. France, Russia, and Britain

    e.   none of the above

Answer: d

3. Among the causes of the Anglo–German rivalry preceding 1914 were
   a. German reactions to the Boer War.
   b. the Fashoda Affair.
   c. competition in the building of naval forces.
   d. economic competition.
   e. a, c, and d only

Answer: e

4. The Bosnian Crisis of 1908 was caused by
   a. Austria-Hungary's annexation of Bosnia-Herzegovina.
   b. Serbia's annexation of Bosnia-Herzegovina.
   c. Bosnia's annexation of Croatia.
   d. the assassination of Archduke Francis Ferdinand of Austria-Hungary.
   e. the Russo-Turkish War of 1907.

Answer: a

5. Social Darwinist thinkers tended to view war as
   a. a "natural" outlet for pent-up aggressive drives.
   b. a legitimate opportunity for nations to gain territory.
   c. a barbaric reversion to outdated practices.
   d. a and b
   e. none of the above

Answer: d

6. The immediate cause of the British declaration of war in 1914 was
   a. Germany's issuing of a "blank check" to Austria-Hungary.
   b. Russian mobilization.
   c. British treaty obligations to France.
   d. German violation of Belgium's neutrality.
   e. the Kruger Telegram.

Answer: d

7. The Schlieffen Plan
   a. was first commissioned by Otto von Bismarck.
   b. proposed a partition of Bosnia.
   c. enraged Serbian nationalists by submitting them to German authority.

    d.   was leaked to Britain by the German traitor Franz Schlieffen.

    e.   none of the above

Answer: e

  8. The Archduke Francis Ferdinand was assassinated by

    a.   a Serbian military officer.

    b.   a Serbian student.

    c.   a Russian secret agent.

    d.   three members of a Bulgarian secret society.

    e.   none of the above

Answer: b

  9. What was the Dreadnought?

    a.   a new German cannon

    b.   a new British warship

    c.   a new British armored vehicle

    d.   a type of British warship renderd obsolete by German submarines

    e.   none of the above

Answer: b

10. The First World War

    a.   surprised most Europeans with its unprecedented bloodshed.

    b.   was greeted with enthusiasm by large numbers of Europeans.

    c.   was deemed inevitable by many Europeans.

    d.   lasted much longer than most Europeans expected.

    e.   all of the above

Answer: e

Short-Answer Questions

  1. What were the principal causes of the First World War? Which of these do you think were the most important, and which do you deem less important? Explain.

  2. What kinds of factors led to the formation of two hostile blocs of Great Powers in Europe around the turn of the century?

  3. Why do you think so many Europeans tended to greet the onset of war with enthusiasm and confidence?

  4. Some Europeans considered World War I an "inevitable" conflict. Do you agree with this assessment? Explain.

5. The peace treaty signed with Germany after the First World War included a famous "war guilt clause" in which Germany accepted primary responsibility, as an aggressor nation, for the conflict. Do you agree that Germany can be singled out as the primary aggressor nation in the years preceding the war, or must the responsibility be more evenly divided among all the major powers? Explain.

True/False Questions

1. The emergence of the Triple Alliance and Triple Entente in the years before 1914 was a factor that brought Europe closer to war.

Answer: T

2. In 1914, Serbia was part of the Austro-Hungarian empire.

Answer: F

3. Serbians regarded Russia as their "natural" ally because of their common Slavic culture.

Answer: T

4. Germany and Austria-Hungary felt confident in 1914 that Italy would support them in an impending war.

Answer: F

5. German diplomacy under Kaiser William II was cautious and conciliatory.

Answer: F

6. German military planners felt confident that Britain would not go to war over the issue of German violation of Belgium's neutrality.

Answer: T

7. Sarajevo was the capital of Serbia.

Answer: F

8. Russian mobilization for war on July 25, 1914, was a major factor precipitating the outbreak of World War I.

Answer: T

9. Britain declared war on Germany before Germany attacked France and Belgium.

Answer: F

10. The French hoped that a victory over Germany would allow them to regain the provinces of Alsace and Lorraine.

Answer: T

Chronology

Place the following items in correct chronological order.

3. Formation of the Triple Alliance
9. Russian mobilization
8. Assassination of Francis Ferdinand
5. Formation of the Triple Entente
1. Franco-Prussian War
10. German attack against France
2. Formation of Three Emperors' League
4. First Moroccan Crisis
6. Bosnian Crisis
7. Second Moroccan Crisis

Part Six
Cataclysm

Chapter 24
The Great War

This chapter narrates the course of World War I, from the opening moves taken by the two sides to the final collapse of the German Empire in November 1918. It also describes the social, economic, and cultural impact that the war exerted upon the belligerent countries themselves.

Chapter Outline

I. The outbreak of war
    A. The Schlieffen Plan
        1. Swift attack in the west, then turn to face Russia's advance
    B. Opening hostilities
        1. The German drive through Belgium
        2. Errors on both sides
        3. German forces reach to within 35 miles of Paris
        4. The Battle of the Marne (September 1914)
        5. The "race for the sea"

II. The changing nature of war
    A. Trench warfare
        1. From the Channel to Switzerland
        2. A total of 6,250 miles of overlapping trenches
        3. Atrocious conditions for soldiers
        4. New technologies, astounding casualties
    B. War in the air and on the seas
        1. Airplanes: from reconnaissance to combat
        2. British command on the seas
        3. Submarine warfare
    C. Support from the home front
        1. Maintaining production levels and morale
        2. Propaganda machines

      3.   Total war, not sparing civilians
      4.   Suppressing political divisions in the name of national unity
      5.   Massive volunteerism in Britain
      6.   Government intervention in regulating the economy and morals
      7.   Key contributions by women

III. A world war
    A.   The eastern front
        1.   Vast Russian reversals (summer 1914)
        2.   Austro-Hungarian losses (September 1914)
        3.   Italy signs the Treaty of London (1915)
    B.   The Middle East, Africa, and the Far East
        1.   The new regime in Turkey sides with Germany
        2.   The disastrous Gallipoli campaign (1915)
        3.   Conflicts in the Balkans
        4.   German colonies conquered by Allies (1914–1916)
    C.   The western front
        1.   German attack fails against Verdun (February 1916)
        2.   British offensive fails on the Somme (July 1916)
    D.   Futility and stalemate
        1.   Millions of dead piling up
        2.   Efforts at a compromise peace fail
    E.   Soldiers and civilians
        1.   Profiteering and resentment
        2.   Censorship conceals true extent of the devastation
        3.   Soldiers' increasing alienation
        4.   Emerging opposition to the war in all the combatant nations
        5.   The Easter Sunday rebellion in Dublin (1916)
        6.   Governments push their populations to hold firm

IV. The final stages
    A.   The United States enters the war
        1.   The sinking of the *Lusitania* (May 1915)
        2.   British success at sea
        3.   The Zimmermann telegram (March 1916)
        4.   Declaration of war (April 6, 1917)
    B.   Russian withdrawal from the war
        1.   Revolution in St. Petersburg (February 1917)
        2.   Kerensky's provisional government
        3.   The Bolshevik Revolution (November 6, 1917)
        4.   The harsh Treaty of Brest-Litovsk (March 1918)

    C. Offensives and mutinies
        1. Growing discontent among rank-and-file soldiers during 1917
        2. Incompetent commanders
        3. The Battle of Paschendaele
        4. Central Powers' success on the Italian front
        5. Allied gains in the Middle East
        6. The Balfour Declaration (November 2, 1917)
    D. The German spring offensive of 1918
        1. Ludendorff's massive attack (March 21, 1918)
        2. After the attack fails, morale plunges in Germany
        3. Austria-Hungary withdraws (November 3, 1918)
    E. The Fourteen Points
        1. President Wilson's speech (January 8, 1918)
        2. An end to secret treaties
        3. Freedom of the seas and of trade
        4. Creation of a League of Nations
        5. Armistice Day (November 11, 1918)

V. The war's impact
    A. Thirty-seven million casualties (8.5 million dead)
        1. Mutilated veterans, impoverished widows
        2. A lost generation
        3. Loss of innocence
        4. Bitter disillusionment

Suggestions for Lecture Topics

A reading of selected passages from the book by Erich Maria Remarque, *All Quiet on the Western Front*, coupled with slides of wartime scenes from the trenches, makes for a gripping lecture on the war's unprecedented brutality.

A lecture on the impact of the war upon European culture and letters can be profitably based on Paul Fussell's *The Great War and Modern Memory*.

For a lecture on the economic and social impact of the war, see Richard Wall and Jay Winter, eds., *The Upheaval of War*.

Two films that deal most poignantly with the war are Jean Renoir's classic *The Grand Illusion*, and Peter Weir's *Gallipoli*. Either one of these films would make an excellent topic for class discussion.

For a lecture on the emergence of pacifism, see Dorothy Jones, *Code of Peace*, and Martin Ceadel, *Pacifism in Britain*.

Multiple-Choice Questions

1. The Schlieffen Plan entailed
    a. simultaneous attacks against France and Russia.
    b. a swift cross-Channel invasion of Britain.
    c. a swift attack against France through Belgium, followed by a turn against Russia.
    d. a swift attack deep into Russia, then a turn back to the west.
    e. alternating attacks of concentrated forces along the western and eastern fronts.

Answer: c

2. The term "sacred union" refers to
    a. the alliance between French and British.
    b. the overcoming of political divisions within each nation.
    c. the alliance between Germans and Austrians.
    d. the secret terms of the Balfour Declaration.
    e. none of the above

Answer: b

3. The Gallipoli campaign took place in
    a. France.
    b. Germany.
    c. Syria.
    d. Turkey.
    e. none of the above

Answer: d

4. The Balfour Declaration
    a. established the conditions for a compromise peace.
    b. established the conditions for an unconditional surrender.
    c. promised British support for Italian colonial aims.
    d. promised British support for the creation of a Jewish homeland.
    e. only b and c

Answer: d

5. Which of the following was NOT one of the principles put forward in the Fourteen Points?
    a. an end to secret treaties
    b. strict limitations on national armaments

    c.   freedom of the seas
    d.   free trade
    e.   creation of a League of Nations

Answer: b

6. Brest–Litovsk was the site of
    a.   a major German military victory.
    b.   a major French victory, after the successful holding of a key fort.
    c.   a major stalemate between British and German troops.
    d.   the principal sea battle of the war.
    e.   a treaty by which Russia exited the war.

Answer: e

7. Which of the following was a strategically crucial town?
    a.   Verdun
    b.   Bordeaux
    c.   Paschendaele
    d.   Ypres
    e.   Gallipoli

Answer: a

8. The Zimmermann telegram
    a.   promised German aid to Irish rebels against Britain.
    b.   promised Italian territorial gains.
    c.   promised the United States financial gains if it stayed neutral.
    d.   promised Mexico territorial gains if it sent troops to fight with Germany in Europe.
    e.   none of the above

Answer: e

9. Which of the following was NOT a major German general?
    a.   Max of Baden
    b.   Ludendorff
    c.   Falkenhayn
    d.   Hindenburg
    e.   Schlieffen

Answer: a

10. Which of the following was NOT a major Allied general?
    a.   Foch

    b.   Clemenceau
    c.   Pétain
    d.   Haig
    e.   Nivelle

Answer: b

Short-Answer Questions

1. What factors contributed to the unprecedented deadliness of the Great War? In what ways was this war different from previous wars?
2. What were the major new technologies through which each side hoped to achieve a decisive "breakthrough"? Why did these technologies fail to achieve what was hoped of them?
3. What was the social impact of the war? For men? For women? For working-class people?
4. What was the cultural impact of the war? What impact did it have on the outlook and worldview of the post-war generation?
5. What does the term "total war" imply? What is different about a "total war," as opposed to the more limited wars of the past?

True/False Questions

1. Trenches on the western front extended from the English Channel all the way to Sweden.

Answer: F

2. Italy entered the war in 1915.

Answer: T

3. The crucial turning point in the war came in 1917.

Answer: T

4. Efforts were made several times to reach a compromise peace.

Answer: T

5. The Treaty of Brest-Litovsk led Russia to cede huge amounts of territory to Germany.

Answer: T

6. The Battle of Paschendaele resulted in a major French defeat.

Answer: F

7. The sinking of the *Lusitania* helped bring the United States into the war.

Answer: T

8. Roger Casement was a British war hero.

Answer: F

9. The war did not officially end until 1922.

Answer: F

10. The Balfour Declaration rejected all attempts at a compromise peace.

Answer: F

Chronology

Place the following items in correct chronological order.
     1. Schlieffen creates plan for two-front war
     3. Italy enters war
     2. Battle of the Marne
     4. Zimmermann telegram
     9. Wilson announces Fourteen Points
     7. Bolshevik Revolution
   10. Armistice (German surrender)
     6. U.S. declaration of war
     5. Easter Sunday rebellion in Dublin
     8. Balfour Declaration

Chapter 25
Revolutionary Russia and the Soviet Union

This chapter surveys the Russian Revolution, from its roots in the tsarist regime to its institutionalization in the Soviet state, from the relative flexibility of the Leninist years to the hardened orthodoxy of the Stalinist dictatorship.

Chapter Outline

I.   The failure of reform and its legacy

II. Unrest, reform, and revolution
   A. A vast and backward nation undergoing rapid industrialization
   B. The movement for reform
      1. By 1914, 100 million peasants, 2.4 million industrial workers
      2. A small labor movement
      3. Strong ties to a traditional social order
      4. A growing professional middle class
   C. Enemies of autocracy
      1. Liberals, populists, and socialists
      2. Founding of (Marxist) Social Democratic Party (1898)
   D. Lenin and the Bolsheviks
      1. Family background
      2. Exile abroad, 1900–1917
      3. The publication of *What Is to Be Done?* (1902)
      4. No compromise with bourgeois parties, strict party discipline
      5. Split between Mensheviks and Bolsheviks (1903)
   E. The Revolution of 1905
      1. A long background of dissent and disgruntlement
      2. The fateful impact of the Russo-Japanese War
      3. Nicholas II convokes a congress of *zemstvos*
      4. Liberals and socialists unite in opposition to autocracy

     5.   "Bloody Sunday" massacre (January 1905)
     6.   Sergei Witte, tsarist proponent of moderate reforms
     7.   The October Manifesto (1905) creates a Duma, or parliament
     8.   Constitutional Democrats (Kadets) seek liberal reforms
     9.   Workers' councils, or soviets, meet in St. Petersburg
    10.   Pogroms of the Black Hundreds
    11.   The Duma's powers eroded by the tsar; Witte dismissed
    12.   Peter Stolypin, the new first minister, seeks rural reforms
    13.   Stolypin's assassination (1911) and the stagnation of reform

III. War and revolution
    A.   Russia at war
        1.   Initial patriotic consensus
        2.   Open opposition to the autocratic regime emerges
        3.   Polarization in Petrograd (wartime name for St. Petersburg)
        4.   Defeats on the battlefield heighten pressures for change
        5.   Tsarina Alexandra and Rasputin
    B.   The Progressive Bloc
        1.   A regime breaking under the pressures of war
        2.   Food shortages peak in 1916–1917
        3.   Police repression of strikes
        4.   Nicholas replaces moderate ministers with reactionaries
    C.   The February Revolution
        1.   Strikes spread in Petrograd early in 1917
        2.   Mutiny among the tsar's soldiers
        3.   Petrograd Soviet of Workers' and Soldiers' Deputies (February 27)
        4.   Nicholas abdicates (March 2)
    D.   The Provisional Government and the Soviet
        1.   Two governments working in parallel
    E.   The army
        1.   Democratization of the military
    F.   The revolution spreads
        1.   Ethnic minorities demand greater self-government
        2.   Nationalism in the Ukraine
        3.   The "All-Russian Conference of Soviets" (March 1917)
        4.   The "April Crisis": pressures for peace
        5.   Radicalization of the workers
    G.   Lenin's return (April 1917)
        1.   The "April Theses"
        2.   The Bolsheviks gain influence

    H. The July Days
        1. Kerensky's ill-fated prosecution of the war
        2. The abortive Bolshevik uprising of July 2
        3. Kerensky's repression of the Bolsheviks
    I. The Kornilov Affair (August 1917)
        1. The specter of a military takeover

IV. The October Revolution
    A. Kerensky's underestimation of Bolshevik influence
    B. The insurrection begins (October 25)
    C. Bolsheviks take power in Petrograd
        1. A relatively bloodless seizure of power
        2. The revolution spreads
        3. Clamping down on opponents on the left
        4. The Bolsheviks consolidate their power
    D. The Peace of Brest-Litovsk
        1. Armistice with Germany (December 1917)
        2. A harshly punitive peace imposed by Germany

V. Civil war
    A. Anti-Bolshevik forces rally and fight
        1. Pogroms in the Ukraine
        2. Famine spreads
    B. Nationalization of major industries
    C. The "Red Terror"
        1. Unlimited powers to the dreaded Cheka
        2. Execution of the tsar and his family
    D. Allied support for the White armies
    E. Triumph of the Red Army

VI. The Soviet Union (created 1922)
    A. A centralized regime replaces the local soviets
    B. The Constitution of July 1918
        1. Freedom of speech and assembly
        2. Separation of church and state
    C. Democratic centralism
        1. Party discipline suffocates democratic initiative from below
        2. Worker strikes against Bolshevik rule (1921)
        3. The Kronstadt Rebellion (March 1921)
    D. The New Economic Policy, or NEP (1921–1928)
        1. Lenin allows some limited market mechanisms

2. Foreign investment sought
3. A concomitant clamping down in the political sphere
E. The rise of Stalin
   1. Georgian background
   2. Quarrels with Trotsky
   3. Lenin's stroke of 1922 and the scramble for succession
   4. Shifting positions on "the national question"
   5. Trotsky mobilizes a "Left Opposition" within the Party
   6. The expulsion of Trotsky from the Party (1929)
F. Five-year plans
   1. Stalin turns to rapid industrialization
   2. The forced collectivization of agriculture (1930)
   3. Bukharin and the "Right Opposition" eliminated by Stalin
   4. The bloodbath in the countryside
   5. Rapid industrialization, and Stakhanovites
   6. The cult of the leader
G. Soviet culture
   1. The culture of utopianism
   2. The cult of technology
   3. The emergence of a repressive orthodoxy in the arts
   4. Religious life in the countryside
H. The purges
   1. Show trials and wild accusations
   2. The Gulag system
   3. Stalin's deepening paranoia
   4. The purge of the military

Suggestions for Lecture Topics

For a lecture on the last years of the tsarist regime, see Marc Ferro, *Nicholas II*.

An excellent account of the 1917 revolution, providing ample material for lectures, is John M. Thompson, *Revolutionary Russia, 1917*.

On Lenin and the Bolsheviks, see Adam Ulam, *The Bolsheviks*.

Two excellent studies of Stalin are Roy Medvedev, *Let History Judge*, and Isaac Deutscher, *Stalin*.

An excellent work that provides detailed background information on the actual functioning of the Soviet system on a day-to-day basis is Moshe Lewin, *The Making of the Soviet System*.

Multiple-Choice Questions

1. The "Kadets" were
   a. conscripts in the army.
   b. conscripts in the navy who rebelled in 1921.
   c. the elite corps of the tsar's personal guard.
   d. a liberal political grouping.
   e. none of the above

Answer: d

2. Sergei Witte was
   a. an adviser to Tsarina Alexandra.
   b. an adviser to Lenin.
   c. a chief minister under Nicholas II.
   d. the man who killed Trotsky.
   e. a priest.

Answer: c

3. The primary reason for the February Revolution was
   a. the chaos produced by the war.
   b. the assassination of Rasputin.
   c. the loss of the Russo-Japanese War.
   d. the massive successes of Bolsheviks in the countryside.
   e. Kerensky's banning of strikes in Petrograd.

Answer: a

4. Peter Stolypin was
   a. a reactionary general.
   b. the tsarina's lover.
   c. the tsar's brother.
   d. a ruthless revolutionary leader.
   e. none of the above

Answer: e

5. Rasputin was
   a. a monk.
   b. Stalin's right-hand man.
   c. a spy.
   d. a character in a Dostoevsky novel.
   e. none of the above

Answer: a

6. The Czech Legion
   a. successfully fought for Czechoslovakia's independence from the U.S.S.R.
   b. was massacred by the Russian army.
   c. fought on the side of the Whites in the Civil War.
   d. fought on the side of the Reds in the Civil War.
   e. held out for 218 days before surrendering to the Red Army in 1928.

Answer: c

7. Kornilov was
   a. a general.
   b. the town where Lenin died.
   c. the town where the Russians withdrew from the First World War.
   d. a peasant leader.
   e. the founder of the Cheka.

Answer: a

8. The NEP
   a. was a dreaded branch of the secret police.
   b. was the last attempt by Nicholas II to stay in power.
   c. was Lenin's pragmatic policy of allowing market reforms.
   d. was Trotsky's group within the Communist Party.
   e. none of the above

Answer: c

9. The first five-year plan began in
   a. 1917.
   b. 1921.
   c. 1924.
   d. 1928.
   e. 1930.

Answer: d

10. Stakhanovites were
    a. elite Russian troops.
    b. labor heroes of the Soviet state.
    c. ruthlessly purged by Stalin in the 1930s.
    d. followers of the religious leader Stakhanov.
    e. a secret cult encouraged by Tsarina Alexandra.

Answer: b

Short-Answer Questions

1. What were the principal causes of the Russian Revolution? Which of these causes do you think were the most important ones? Explain.
2. If you had been in Kerensky's place, what would you have done differently? Explain.
3. Why is Lenin sometimes referred to as a brilliant tactician? On what occasions, specifically, did he show flexibility and shrewd tactical sense?
4. Do you think the dictatorship of Stalin's era was inevitable? Might a different leadership have moved the Communist revolution toward a more humane path of action? Explain.
5. Why did the advent of a Communist regime in Russia take many Marxists by surprise? What were the long-term effects of the fact that the world's first Communist state was created on the ashes of the Russian Empire?

True/False Questions

1. Lenin accepted Brest-Litovsk because he thought a revolution was imminent in Germany.

Answer: T

2. Trotsky was murdered by an agent of Stalin's.

Answer: T

3. The "April Theses" pertained to Nicholas II's abdication.

Answer: F

4. The Kronstadt Rebellion was one of the first signs of the tsar's downfall.

Answer: F

5. The NEP allowed for capitalist enterprise in the Communist state.

Answer: T

6. Bukharin was a leader of the "Right Opposition."

Answer: T

7. The Cheka was the forerunner of the K.G.B.

Answer: T

8. Stalin's real name was Sergei Duma.

Answer: F

9. The United States, Britain, and France sent money and troops to help the White generals in their attempt to crush the Bolsheviks.

Answer: T

10. Stalin was Party Secretary for the Communist Party during the 1920s.

Answer: T

Chronology

Place the following items in correct chronological order.
1. Founding of the Russian Social Democratic Party
8. End of NEP
4. Kerensky flees Russia
3. February Revolution
2. Russo-Japanese War
6. End of Civil War
7. Lenin dies
5. Kronstadt Rebellion
10. Stalinist purges
9. Collectivization of agriculture

Chapter 26
The Elusive Search for Stability in the 1920s

This chapter describes the Peace of Paris of 1919 and its consequences, then surveys the years of political and economic instability that followed. It closes with a description of the rise of fascism in Italy and Germany.

Chapter Outline

I. The resolution of the war
  A. Revolution in Germany and Hungary
    1. The collapse of the German Empire
    2. A new republic, under siege from left and right
    3. Challenges to the new socialist government
    4. Béla Kun's Communist experiment in Hungary
  B. The Treaty of Versailles
    1. The Big Four: Lloyd George, Clemenceau, Wilson, Orlando
    2. Conflicting aims of the Great Powers
    3. France's bitter quest for security
    4. Britain's role as a balancer
    5. Italian irredentism
    6. Wilson's idealism
    7. Article 231, the "war guilt clause"
    8. The harsh conditions imposed on Germany
    9. The festering sore of reparations
    10. The toothless League of Nations
    11. Exclusion of Soviet Russia from the peacemaking
  C. Settlements in Eastern Europe
    1. The treaties of Trianon, Neuilly, and Sèvres
    2. Atatürk's resistance leads to the Treaty of Lausanne (1923)

II. Instability in the post-war world

    A. The national question
        1. A bewildering array of new nations in Central Europe
        2. Religious differences and ethnic rivalries
        3. The Little Entente (1921)
        4. The ethnic congeries of Yugoslavia
        5. Tensions in Czechoslovakia
        6. Poland turns toward dictatorship under Pilsudski
        7. Bloodshed in the Balkans
    B. Colonial questions
        1. The "mandate system" of the League
        2. Conflict in Palestine
        3. Ireland gains independence (1922), with the exception of Ulster
        4. The British Commonwealth
        5. Britain resists Indian claims to self-rule
        6. Japan emerges as a Great Power
    C. Social tensions in Europe
        1. The war's legacy: inflation and unemployment
        2. Class polarization mounts
        3. Women gain the right to vote in some European nations
        4. Conservatives in Britain and France rally against working class
        5. The spread of trade unions in Europe

III. Post-war politics and economy
    A. The fragile Weimar Republic
        1. Leftist insurrections in Bavaria (1919–1920)
        2. The Kapp Putsch (1920)
        3. Walther Rathenau and the Treaty of Rapallo (1922)
        4. Hyperinflation and the French invasion of the Ruhr (1923)
        5. Gustav Stresemann's shrewd diplomacy
        6. The Dawes Plan (1924) and Treaty of Locarno (1925)
    B. Reformists and revolutionaries
        1. Socialist internationalism re-emerges after the war
        2. The French Socialists' Congress of Tours (1920)
        3. Léon Blum and the new Socialist Party
        4. The hard-line French Communist Party grows dramatically
        5. The widespread success of the reformist stance
        6. An emerging model: the welfare state
    C. The established democracies: Britain and France
        1. Class polarization in Britain
        2. Labour Party successes, at the expense of the Liberals

    3. Economic doldrums
    4. The general strike (1926)
    5. Conservatives dominate French post-war politics
    6. Instability of the franc
  D. Artists and intellectuals
    1. Defiant modernism: the "lost generation"
    2. Dada
    3. Expressionism
    4. The surrealists explore the irrational

IV. The rise of fascism
  A. Mussolini's rise in Italy
    1. Irredentism and the Fiume crisis (1919)
    2. Mussolini's background
    3. Crisis of Italy's liberal state amid economic turmoil
    4. The "red scare" of 1920–1922
    5. The fascist ideology
    6. The "march on Rome" (1922)
    7. The consolidation of power
    8. The Lateran Pacts with the Vatican
  B. Hitler and Nazis in Germany
    1. Austrian origins and early years
    2. Spengler's *Decline of the West*
    3. Hitler joins the German Workers' Party (1919)
    4. The Beer Hall Putsch (1923)
    5. Hitler writes *Mein Kampf*
    6. The cult of the Führer
    7. Support for the Nazis from a broad spectrum of the population
    8. The decisive impact of the Great Depression

Suggestions for Lecture Topics

A reading of T. S. Eliot's poem, "The Hollow Men," can forcefully convey to students the sense of cynicism and bitterness that followed the war.

It is a good idea to devote an entire lecture to the distinction between reformists and revolutionaries in the European left; otherwise, students tend to lump together the SPD and KPD, the French socialists and Communists, the Spartacists and anarchists, all under the single rubric of the "reds." See George Lichtheim, *Marxism*, for a lucid treatment of the subject.

Modernism in the arts fascinates students, since it is still in many ways a form of art that remains prevalent today, and yet strikes many students as alien and bizarre. One way to approach the subject is to create a multimedia presentation, with slides of art works, readings from literature (such as André Breton and James Joyce), and selections of music (juxtaposing, in succession, works by Mozart, Stravinsky, and Webern or Berg). Students tend to respond vigorously if they are asked to discuss and comment on these works, and to link them to their historical context. For a superb book on this subject, implicitly referred to by Merriman in the text, see Peter Gay, *Weimar Culture: The Outsider as Insider.*

For a lecture on the Franco-German conflict after the Great War, see Walter McDougall, *France's Rhineland Diplomacy.*

A good general work on the emergence of fascism is F. L. Carsten, *The Rise of Fascism.*

Multiple-Choice Questions

1. Béla Kun was
   a. the castle where Germany signed the armistice for World War I.
   b. the German foreign minister who negotiated the Locarno Treaty.
   c. a Czech philosopher.
   d. a Hungarian Communist.
   e. an Italian fascist.

Answer: d

2. Which of the following was NOT one of the Big Four at Paris in 1919?
   a. Lloyd George
   b. Churchill
   c. Orlando
   d. Wilson
   e. Clemenceau

Answer: b

3. Which of the following was NOT one of the treaties of the Peace of Paris of 1919?
   a. Trianon
   b. Neuilly
   c. Boulogne-Billancourt
   d. Sèvres
   e. Versailles

Answer: c

4. The Treaty of Rapallo
   a. arranged for secret military cooperation between Germany and the Soviet Union.
   b. dealt with Italian designs on Dalmatia.
   c. promised the Jews a homeland in Palestine.
   d. formally created the state of Poland.
   e. none of the above

Answer: a

5. The Dawes Plan
   a. arranged for secret payments to British generals.
   b. arranged for U.S. loans to Germany.
   c. helped stabilize the French currency.
   d. was a result of the Locarno Conference.
   e. created a schedule for German reparations payments.

Answer: b

6. Léon Blum was
   a. a French financier.
   b. a French Socialist.
   c. a Polish aristocrat.
   d. a Jewish spy.
   e. a Jewish diplomat.

Answer: b

7. The General Strike of 1926 was crushed by
   a. Macdonald.
   b. Lloyd George.
   c. Churchill.
   d. Pétain.
   e. Clemenceau.

Answer: c

8. The surrealists were most strongly influenced by
   a. Hegel.
   b. Nietzsche.
   c. Einstein.
   d. Freud.
   e. Heidegger.

Answer: d

9. The Fiume Crisis
   a. began when the poet D'Annunzio invaded Rome.
   b. centered on the status of Jews in Italy.
   c. gave Mussolini his first major victory.
   d. centered on the legal status of a city on the Adriatic coast.
   e. was the banking scandal that helped propel Mussolini into power.

Answer: d

10. Gustav Stresemann
   a. signed the Versailles Treaty for Germany.
   b. was murdered by Free Corps soldiers.
   c. failed to prevent hyperinflation.
   d. resigned under pressure from Hitler.
   e. none of the above

Answer: e

Short-Answer Questions

1. What were the conflicting aims of the Big Four at Versailles, and how did these conflicting aims contribute to the shaping of the peace?
2. Describe the conflict the led up to the French invasion of the Ruhr and its implications for European diplomacy. How was this Franco-German conflict resolved?
3. What were the weaknesses of the Weimar Republic, and how were they exploited by Hitler?
4. What were some of the main points of the ideology of fascism? What factors rendered this ideology attractive to many Europeans in the aftermath of the Great War?
5. What is meant by "modernism" in the arts? How is modernism exemplified in the currents of dadaism, expressionism, and surrealism? Explain.

True/False Questions

1. Article 231 of the Treaty of Versailles placed all the blame for the Great War on Germany.

Answer: T

2. Atatürk's resistance to the stipulations of the Peace of Paris was ultimately successful.

Answer: T

3. Poland was the first European country to fall back into dictatorship after the war.

Answer: T

4. Mussolini took power through a violent coup d'état.

Answer: F

5. Hitler was not born in Germany but in Austria.

Answer: T

6. The Treaty of Neuilly dealt with Poland.

Answer: F

7. In Germany in 1923, an apple could cost a billion marks.

Answer: T

8. The Vatican gave its full moral and legal approval to Mussolini's dictatorship.

Answer: T

9. The first Labour Party Prime Minister of Britain was Lloyd George.

Answer: F

10. All of Ireland, including Ulster, became independent from Great Britain in 1922.

Answer: F

Chronology

Place the following items in correct chronological order.
   6. Beer Hall Putsch
   4. Kapp Putsch
   5. Ireland gains independence
   1. Bolshevik Revolution

7. Dawes Plan
3. Fiume Crisis
9. General Strike
10. Lateran Pacts
8. Locarno Conference
2. End of Great War

Chapter 27
The Europe of Depression and Dictatorship

This chapter describes the grim 1930s—the Great Depression, the spread of fascist movements throughout Europe, the consolidation of Nazi power in Germany, the Spanish Civil War, and the spiral of Nazi aggression leading to the Second World War.

Chapter Outline

I. Economies in crisis
    A. The Great Depression
        1. The 1924–1929 interlude of superficial prosperity
        2. The impending crisis of agriculture
        3. Tariff barriers and indebtedness
        4. Financial speculation
        5. The collapse of the New York stock market (October 1929)
        6. The strong link between the U.S. and the German economies
        7. Mass unemployment
        8. Collapse of the international monetary system
        9. The National Government in Britain (1931) ends gold standard
        10. Failure of deflationary measures
        11. Mosley and the British fascists
        12. France, after holding out two years, succumbs to hard times
    B. Gradual revival
        1. Keynes proposes deficit spending to stimulate economies
        2. Lingering depression in France and the U.S.

II. Fascist movements
    A. A wide variety of movements, united by anti-communism and anti-Semitism
    B. The dynamics of fascism

      1. Middle-class frustrations
      2. Fears of working-class power
      3. Support from big business interests
      4. The weakness of parliamentary democracy
      5. The appeal of a more powerful state structure
      6. The appealing ideology of "national community"
      7. Corporatist economies
      8. The legacy of the Great War
      9. Racism and aggressive nationalism

C. Mussolini's Italy
      1. Posing as a third way between capitalism and communism
      2. The National Council of Corporations
      3. Economic independence
      4. Heavy military spending
      5. Eliminating the boundary between public and private life
      6. Resistance and indifference among sections of the population

D. Fascist movements in Eastern Europe
      1. A backward, conflict-ridden region (Czechoslovakia excepted)
      2. Falling like dominoes into dicatatorship
      3. Bitter polarization between left and right in Austria
      4. Dollfuss moves toward dictatorship by 1933

E. The French Popular Front
      1. Popularity of fascist leagues and organizations in France
      2. The hated Third Republic
      3. Virulent anti-Semitism
      4. The Popular Front: Radicals, Socialists, Communists (1934)
      5. The Popular Front's electoral victory (1936)
      6. "Better Hitler than Blum!"
      7. Fascists in Belgium

III. Nazism
  A. The collapse of Weimar democracy
      1. The shattering impact of the Great Depression
      2. Rapid rise in electoral success of extreme left and right
      3. Traditional conservatives throw their support to Hitler
      4. The intimidation campaigns of the Nazi SA (Stormtroopers)
      5. Feckless maneuvering between Papen and Schleicher
      6. Fatal underestimation of Hitler
      7. Hitler's legal entry into power (January 30, 1933)
  B. Nazi totalitarianism

      1. A ruthlessly rapid consolidation of power
      2. The Reichstag fire and the Enabling Act (March 1933)
      3. Banning of political parties
      4. Systematic dismantling of democratic institutions
      5. Hitler crushes Röhm's SA on "night of the long knives" (1934)
      6. The Nazi program of "coordination" throughout civil society
      7. The "leadership principle"
      8. The organization of leisure: Strength through Joy
      9. The subordination of women
     10. Hitler and the intellectuals
     11. Goebbels and the art of propaganda
  C. The Third Reich and the Jews
      1. The Nuremberg Laws (1935)
      2. Emigration of many Jews, hampered by growing restrictions
      3. *Kristallnacht* (November 9, 1938)
  D. Hitler's foreign policy
      1. Limitless and megalomaniacal aims
      2. "Living space" to be conquered in the east
      3. A shrewdly calculated policy: "break the chains of Versailles"
      4. A cynical non-aggression pact with Poland (January 1934)
  E. Hitler and Mussolini
      1. Mussolini's aims of aggrandizement
      2. The assassination of Dollfuss (1934)
      3. Hitler's first attempt at *Anschluss* with Austria fails
      4. Hitler announces rearmament (1935)
      5. Italian invasion of Ethiopia (1935)
      6. The League of Nations imposes weak sanctions on Italy
  F. Remilitarization
      1. German troops reoccupy the Rhineland (March 1936)
      2. Massive arms buildup by Hitler spurs European arms race

IV. The Spanish Civil War
  A. Social and political instability
      1. An ineffectual king and a military dictator during the 1920s
      2. Birth of the republic (1931)
      3. Left-right polarization, marked by escalating violence
      4. Military insurrection begins in 1936
      5. Tensions among the defenders of the republic
      6. Nationalist rebels rally behind Francisco Franco
  B. Loyalists versus nationalists

1. A savage and merciless struggle
2. International Brigades
3. Germany and Italy send aid to Franco
4. Collapse of the Republic (1939)
5. Franco establishes an authoritarian dictatorship

V. The coming of World War II
   A. The Axis
      1. Italy and Germany join forces (1936)
      2. Mussolini adopts Hitler's anti-Semitism
      3. Japanese expansionism in the 1930s
      4. Japan signs friendship treaty with Germany (1936)
   B. Aggression and appeasement
      1. Hitler moves into Austria (1938)
      2. Hitler's designs on the Czech Sudetenland
      3. Frenzied diplomacy by Britain's Neville Chamberlain
      4. France and Britain sell out Czechoslovakia at Munich (1938)
      5. Hitler breaks the Munich agreements by occupying Czechoslovakia
      6. Hitler turns to Poland
      7. The Pact of Steel between Germany and Italy (1939)
      8. The Nazi-Soviet Pact stuns the world (August 21, 1939)
      9. Hitler invades Poland (September 1, 1939) and war begins

Suggestions for Lecture Topics

For a lecture on the Great Depression, see Charles Kindleberger, *The World in Depression*.

An excellent study of the consolidation of Nazi power in a small German town, full of concrete examples upon which to draw for a lecture, is William S. Allen, *The Nazi Seizure of Power*.

Recent scholarship on the Nazi regime is exemplified by Ian Kershaw, *The Hitler Myth*, and Detlev Peukert, *Inside Nazi Germany*.

For a lecture on the Spanish Civil War see Hugh Thomas, *The Spanish Civil War*.

On the years leading up to war, see Donald Watt, *How War Came*. For a broad, comparative study of fascism, see Stanley Payne, *Fascism*, and Carl Friedrich and Zbigniew Brzezinski, *Totalitarian Dictatorship and Autocracy*.

Multiple-Choice Questions

1. Which country felt the effects of the Great Depression later than all the others?
   a. Sweden
   b. United States
   c. France
   d. Germany
   e. Great Britain

Answer: c

2. Which of the following was NOT a factor in the dynamics of fascism?
   a. fears of communism
   b. strong internationalist sympathies
   c. the perceived weaknesses of parliamentary democracy
   d. the bitter legacy of the Great War
   e. racism

Answer: b

3. Which of the following countries did NOT succumb to authoritarian government during the interwar years?
   a. Czechoslovakia
   b. Poland
   c. Hungary
   d. Romania
   e. Yugoslavia

Answer: a

4. Which of the following were NOT members of the French Popular Front?
   a. Radicals
   b. Action Française
   c. Socialists
   d. Communists

Answer: b

5. Which of the following was NOT involved in the political struggles that immediately preceded Hitler's appointment to the position of chancellor?
   a. Papen
   b. Schleicher

   c. Hindenburg
   d. Rathenau
   e. none of the above

Answer: d

6. The "night of the long knives" was
   a. the night on which an anti-Semitic pogrom swept through Germany.
   b. the night before the *Anschluss* with Austria.
   c. the night in which Hitler crushed Röhm's SA.
   d. the night before the invasion of Poland.
   e. the night of Dollfuss's assassination.

Answer: c

7. Goebbels was
   a. Hitler's secretary.
   b. the head of the SS.
   c. the head of the SA.
   d. the head of the Gestapo.
   e. propaganda chief.

Answer: e

8. In what year did the Munich Conference take place?
   a. 1933
   b. 1936
   c. 1937
   d. 1938
   e. 1939

Answer: d

9. Which of the following countries sent aid to the democratic defenders of the republic during the Spanish Civil War?
   a. the United States
   b. France
   c. Britain
   d. the Soviet Union
   e. none of the above

Answer: d

10. The Sudetenland
   a. was part of Czechoslovakia, coveted by Poland.

b. was part of Czechoslovakia, coveted by Hungary.
c. was part of Poland, coveted by Germany.
d. was part of Yugoslavia, coveted by Italy.
e. none of the above

Answer: e

Short-Answer Questions

1. What were the main causes of the Great Depression? Why did it last as long as it did?
2. What were some of the main reasons for the appeal of fascism in Europe?
3. What was entailed in the Nazi program of "coordination" for Germany? Give a reasonably detailed account of what this term meant in practice.
4. Why was the Spanish Civil War seen as a test case, or dress rehearsal, for the Second World War? Describe the principal forces involved in the conflict, the stakes involved, and the international ramifications of the conflict.
5. What motivated the "appeasement" of Munich? Apart from the desire for peace, what sorts of calculations and hopes animated Chamberlain and Daladier? Do you think they were completely wrong in entertaining such hopes, or were they only wrong in applying these hopes to the wrong man at the wrong time?

True/False Questions

1. Even before the U.S. stock market crash, a serious crisis of world agriculture was already on the horizon.

Answer: T

2. Britain had its own fascist party.

Answer: T

3. Anti-Semitism was weak in Europe during the 1930s, with the sole exception of Germany.

Answer: F

4. Léon Blum was the first Jew to hold the post of prime minister in France.

Answer: T

5. Hitler became chancellor in Germany through legal channels.

Answer: T

6. Hitler became chancellor in 1934.

Answer: F

7. The Italian invasion of Ethiopia was a failure.

Answer: F

8. The Nuremberg Laws expelled Jews from Germany.

Answer: F

9. Franco received aid from Hitler and Mussolini.

Answer: T

10. Austen Chamberlain orchestrated the appeasement of Germany at Munich.

Answer: F

Chronology

Place the following items in correct chronological order.
   10. Nazi–Soviet Pact
   8. Popular Front victory in France
   2. Beginning of Great Depression
   3. Creation of National Government in Britain
   4. Hitler becomes chancellor
   7. Nuremberg Laws
   9. German *Anschluss* with Austria
   6. Night of the Long Knives
   1. Locarno Treaty
   5. Enabling Act

Chapter 28

World War II

This chapter surveys the course of the Second World War, describing both the military campaigns and the socioeconomic aspects of the conflict.

Chapter Outline

I. The war in Europe begins
  A. The German invasion of Poland (September 1, 1939)
    1. The nature of *Blitzkrieg*
    2. The Soviets attack from the east
  B. The "Phony War"
    1. French troops hunker down behind the Maginot Line
    2. Hitler puts off attack until the spring
  C. The war in the frozen north
    1. The Finns' brave "winter war" against the Soviets
    2. Denmark surrenders to the Nazis without a fight
    3. A Nazi puppet government under Quisling in Norway
    4. Chamberlain replaced by Churchill (May 10, 1940)
  D. The fall of France
    1. Demoralization among the French defenders
    2. The German attack in the west begins (May 10, 1940)
    3. A stunningly rapid military collapse
    4. Marshal Philippe Pétain becomes the new French premier
  E. The Battle of Britain
    1. Struggling for control of the skies
    2. Hitler deterred from invasion

II. A global war
  A. Total war
    1. U.S. aid to Britain, via Lend-Lease (March 1941)
    2. A massive effort, coordinated by government

3.   New technologies
B.   Hitler's allies
   1.   The alliance with Japan
   2.   Spain's neutrality
   3.   Romania, Hungary, and Bulgaria eventually join the Axis
   4.   Italian military incompetence
C.   The German invasion of Russia
   1.   The fateful delay caused by the campaign in the Balkans
   2.   The German drive eastward begins (June 22, 1941)
   3.   After initial success, the Germans encounter stiff resistance
   4.   The Germans bog down in the dead of winter
D.   Pearl Harbor
   1.   The background of Japanese expansionism
   2.   The attack comes (December 7, 1941)
   3.   Japanese successes in the Pacific
   4.   U.S. declaration of war, and German declaration of war on U.S.
   5.   Internment of Japanese-Americans
   6.   British-American coordination of their war efforts

III.   Hitler's Europe
A.   The Nazi "New European Order"
   1.   German treatment of areas under occupation
B.   The "Final Solution"
   1.   The execution of 70,000 handicapped Germans
   2.   Plans to exterminate Jews and decimate Slavs
   3.   The world of the death camps
   4.   Collaboration among Germany's allies
   5.   Occasional cases of resistance and saving of Jews
   6.   The barbaric experiments of the Nazi doctors
   7.   Questions about intervention to stop the Holocaust
C.   Resistance to the Nazis
   1.   Tito in Yugoslavia
   2.   Croatian fascists murder 300,000 Serbs
   3.   The Vichy regime in France
   4.   The role of Vichy in rounding up Jews for the Nazis
   5.   De Gaulle and Free France
   6.   Jean Moulin and the Resistance network in France
D.   Against Hitler in Germany
   1.   The vast majority remain loyal to the Führer until the end
   2.   The effectiveness of the SS and Gestapo

       3.   A dissident subculture among a small minority of youths
       4.   Stauffenberg and the plot to kill Hitler (July 20, 1944)

IV. The tide turns
    A.   Germany on the defensive
       1.   Speer triples German war output
    B.   The war in North Africa
       1.   Rommel versus Montgomery in the desert
       2.   Stalin's demands for a second front in the west
       3.   Churchill's preference for a gradual attack from the south
       4.   Darlan versus de Gaulle
       5.   The Axis routed from northern Africa
       6.   Strategic bombing of Germany
    C.   Hitler's Russian disaster
       1.   The German army's supply problem
       2.   The Red Army grows in effectiveness
       3.   The siege of Leningrad (506 days)
       4.   The Battle of Stalingrad (ended February 2, 1943)
    D.   The Allied invasion of Italy
       1.   A strike northward through Sicily (July 1943)
       2.   Mussolini deposed
       3.   Mussolini rescued by Hitler, heads "Italian Social Republic"
    E.   The Big Three
       1.   The Casablanca meeting of January 1943
       2.   The Teheran Conference of November 1943
    F.   The invasion of France
       1.   June 6, 1944: the long-awaited D-Day landing in Normandy
       2.   De Gaulle enters Paris (August 25)
       3.   The Battle of the Bulge
       4.   Hitler's last-ditch technology: the V-1 and V-2

V. Allied victory
    A.   The Churchill-Stalin meeting of October 1944
    B.   Yalta (February 1945)
       1.   Spheres of occupation of Germany
       2.   The post-war government of Poland
       3.   The United Nations
    C.   The end of Mussolini and Hitler
    D.   The German surrender (May 8, 1945)
    E.   The defeat of Japan
       1.   A vast naval theater of war

    2.   The bombing campaign over Japan
    3.   Hiroshima (August 6, 1945)
    4.   Japan's surrender (September 2, 1945)
F.   The war's end
    1.   The Holocaust unveiled to the world
    2.   37 million dead, half in the Soviet Union
    3.   Questions about guilt and responsibility

Suggestions for Lecture Topics

For a lecture on the social and economic aspects of the war, an older but still outstanding source is Gordon Wright, *The Ordeal of Total War.*

On the French defeat in 1940, see the profound essay by the eminent French historian Marc Bloch, *Strange Defeat*, which was written in 1940 shortly before the author was captured and tortured to death by the Nazis for his role in the anti-fascist resistance. On the Vichy regime, see Robert Paxton, *Vichy France.*

For a lecture on the Holocaust the most comprehensive source is Raul Hilberg, *The Destruction of the European Jews.* Students may also be interested in the film *Obedience,* based on the famous experiments conducted at Yale University in the 1960s; the film makes a powerful starting point for a discussion about the continuing relevance of the Holocaust in today's world.

For a lecture on the advent of the nuclear age, an excellent source is the Pulitzer-prize-winning book by Richard Rhodes, *The Making of the Atomic Bomb.*

Two extremes of human conduct during the war, which make a gripping combination for a lecture, are depicted in Philip Hallie, *Lest Innocent Blood Be Shed* and Christopher Browning, *Ordinary Men.* The former tells the story of a group of villagers in south-central France who saved the lives of some 5,000 Jews; the latter narrates the deeds of a group of German army reservists who systematically massacred Jews in occupied Poland.

Multiple-Choice Questions

1. Vidkun Quisling was
    a.   a Russian spy.
    b.   a Norwegian fascist.
    c.   a Swedish Nazi.

    d.   a Danish Resistance leader.

    e.   a Finnish traitor.

Answer: b

2. The major turning point in the war, in which the Axis first began to decline in power, and the Allies began to gain the upper hand, was
   a. late in 1941.
   b. in 1943.
   c. early in 1944.
   d. late in 1944.
   e. early in 1945.

Answer: b

3. The term "Phony War" referred to
   a. the skirmishes between Italians and Albanians in 1941.
   b. the Italian invasion of France after France's defeat by the Germans.
   c. the lull in fighting during the winter of 1939–1940.
   d. U.S. aid to the British before the U.S. had formally entered the war.
   e. none of the above

Answer: c

4. The role of the Vichy regime in the Holocaust was
   a. active initiative in the rounding up of Jews for the Germans.
   b. reluctant cooperation with the Germans.
   c. sullen resistance to the Germans.
   d. defiant opposition to the Germans.
   e. establishment of death camps within French territory.

Answer: a

5. The Holocaust
   a. was not discovered until after the German surrender.
   b. was known about outside Germany only by a few Jewish leaders.
   c. was carried out openly by the Germans.
   d. was well documented and known about by Allied leaders by 1943.
   e. was well documented and known about by Allied leaders by 1940.

Answer: d

6. The nation that suffered the highest number of dead and wounded in the war was
   a. Germany.

  b. Japan.
  c. France.
  d. Britain.
  e. none of the above

Answer: e

7. Jean Moulin was
  a. a Resistance leader.
  b. a general.
  c. a traitor.
  d. a Vichy politician.
  e. the assistant to General de Gaulle.

Answer: a

8. The secret Churchill-Stalin meeting of October 1944 dealt with
  a. Britain's colonial future.
  b. the future of the British Communist Party.
  c. future spheres of influence in Central Europe.
  d. military plans for D-Day.
  e. none of the above

Answer: c

9. Stauffenberg was
  a. the man who tried to kill Hitler.
  b. a brilliant Nazi propagandist.
  c. a German film-maker.
  d. a German general.
  e. a secret spy for the British.

Answer: a

10. D-Day occurred on
  a. August 6, 1943.
  b. September 6, 1943.
  c. June 6, 1944.
  d. February 6, 1945.
  e. none of the above

Answer: c

Short-Answer Questions

1. What were the principal reasons for the stunningly rapid collapse of France in 1940?
2. What role did the "Final Solution" play in Hitler's vision of the future of the Third Reich?
3. What, in your opinion, were the most decisive mistakes made by Hitler in his prosecution of the war? Explain your answers briefly.
4. What were the basic reasons for the outbreak of the Second World War? In what ways might this war be seen as related to the First World War?
5. Describe the conflicting aims of Britain, the Soviet Union, and the United States, as their leaders met at Teheran in 1943 and then again at Yalta in 1945.

True/False Questions

1. The Battle of the Bulge was won by the Germans.

Answer: F

2. The word *Blitzkrieg* means "thunder strike" in German.

Answer: F

3. Initially, Charles de Gaulle was spurned by Churchill and Roosevelt.

Answer: T

4. The Nazis killed not only Jews, but also German citizens who were considered Aryan but "unfit."

Answer: T

5. The Vichy regime in France refused to cooperate with the Holocaust.

Answer: F

6. Mussolini committed suicide in 1945.

Answer: F

7. Most Germans remained loyal to Hitler to the bitter end.

Answer: T

8. Spain remained neutral in the war.

Answer: T

9. Romania, Hungary, and Finland joined the Axis powers by 1941.

Answer: F

10. Croatian fascists murdered 300,000 Serbs during the war.

Answer: T

Chronology

Place the following items in correct chronological order.
  8. German surrender
  4. Churchill becomes prime minister
  5. Pearl Harbor
  7. Plot to kill Hitler fails
 10. Japanese surrender
  2. German invasion of Poland
  9. Hiroshima bombing
  3. Winter War in Finland
  6. Battle of Stalingrad
  1. Nazi-Soviet Pact

Part Seven

Europe in the
Post-War Era

Chapter 29
Rebuilding Divided Europe

This chapter describes Europe's recovery from the devastation of World War II, the political realignments that followed this global military conflict, the bloody struggles of decolonization, the cultural and economic changes of a rapidly modernizing post-war society, and the major superpower confrontations that marked the first two decades of post-war history.

Chapter Outline

I. Europe at the end of the war
   A. Higher casualties than World War I
   B. Much of Europe devastated
   C. The Potsdam Settlement (July 1945)
      1. New national boundaries and territorial adjustments
      2. Control over Germany by the U.S., U.S.S.R., France, and Britain
      3. Growing mistrust between the Western Allies and Soviet Union
      4. The dawn of the nuclear era, and its attendant tensions
      5. Soviet reparations from Germany
   D. The United Nations and Cold War Alliances
      1. The Dumbarton Oaks Conference (November 1944)
      2. Structure and membership
      3. NATO vs. the Warsaw Pact
   E. Economic and social turmoil
      1. Wartime destruction, weakened economies
      2. Refugee problems on a vast scale
      3. Punishment of Nazi collaborators varies from nation to nation
      4. The Nuremberg trials
   F. Intellectual currents
      1. Widespread pessimism among intellectuals
      2. The lure of communism
      3. Existentialism: Camus and Sartre

    4. The "theater of the absurd"
    5. Intellectuals and the Third World
    6. State-controlled intellectual life in the Soviet sphere
    7. A renaissance of European cinema

II. Political realignments
    A. Truman Doctrine and Marshall Plan (1947)
    B. Divided Germany
        1. Birth of the Federal Republic of Germany under Allied tutelage
        2. Konrad Adenauer's central role in West German politics
        3. Swift reintegration of West Germany into Western Europe
        4. Soviet-dominated German Democratic Republic (G.D.R.) in the East
    C. Eastern Europe under the Soviet shadow
        1. Communist takeovers in Hungary, Romania, Bulgaria, and Poland
        2. The failure of Beneš and Masaryk to save Czech democracy
        3. Stalinist purges and iron discipline imposed from Moscow
        4. Yugoslavia: successful resistance to Soviet domination
        5. The defeat of the Greek Communists with British and U.S. aid
    D. Labour's victory in Britain
        1. A stunning upset victory for Labour
        2. Building a welfare state, despite severe economic limitations
        3. Conservatives return to power in 1951, but keep welfare state
    E. A new republic in France
        1. De Gaulle's interregnum, 1944–1946
        2. Strong showing by the left
        3. A constitution crafted to ensure a weak executive
        4. State-governed economic recovery
    F. Italy ends the monarchy
        1. Voters approve a constitution for a decentralized state
        2. The crucial legacy of the Resistance
        3. Fundamentally different experiences, north and south
        4. Staunchly anti-Communist government under Christian Democrats
        5. The "economic miracle" of the 1950s
    G. Politics in the Soviet Union
        1. Stalin at the peak of his dictatorial power and his paranoia
        2. Collective leadership after Stalin's death in 1953
        3. Nikita Khrushchev emerges in 1955 as "first among equals"

4. A new emphasis on consumer goods
5. Khrushchev's secret speech of 1956, denouncing Stalin's crimes
6. The police state lives on, overseeing a badly faltering economy

III. Decolonization
   A. India and Southeast Asia
      1. A long background of Indian agitation for self-rule
      2. Attlee announces imminent independence for India in 1946
      3. Hindu-Muslim conflicts, and the partition of 1947
      4. A daunting array of social and economic problems
      5. Independence movements in Southeast Asia
      6. Sukarno and Suharto in Indonesia
   B. Britain and the Middle East
      1. Declining British influence
      2. Division of Palestine into Israel and Jordan
      3. War leaves Palestinians homeless
      4. Mounting Israeli-Arab hostility
   C. The Suez Canal Crisis
      1. Strategic importance of the canal
      2. Struggles between Britain and rising Egyptian nationalists
      3. Nasser strengthens ties with Soviets and nationalizes canal
      4. Anglo-French-Israeli forces attack Egypt
      5. The attack fails, because of strong pressure from superpowers
      6. British influence in the Middle East rapidly declines
   D. French decolonization
      1. Ho Chi Minh and Vietnamese nationalism
      2. The crushing French defeat at Dien Bien Phu (1954)
      3. Division of Vietnam into two halves
      4. Anticolonial movements in northern Africa
      5. A bitter war develops in Algeria amid increasing controversy
      6. Rumors of a military coup in Paris prompt de Gaulle's return
      7. Birth of the Fifth Republic (1958)
      8. De Gaulle moves to grant Algeria independence (1962)
      9. A resolutely independent "third force" foreign policy
   E. Decolonization in Africa
      1. Apartheid in South Africa
      2. Ethnic and tribal rivalries breed conflict in the Congo
      3. Marxist influence in Mozambique

IV. Economic and social changes
   A. Economic recovery and the welfare state

    1. Post-war cooperation and reconstruction
    2. The emergence of supranational organizations in Western Europe
    3. A vast increase in social services provided by the state
    4. Rising standards of living
  B. Economic growth in the West
    1. Housing as a high priority in the aftermath of war
    2. Rapid growth, large corporations
    3. A transformation of the workforce
    4. Germany and Japan as the economic giants of the post-war era
    5. The key role of Marshall Plan aid
    6. Mixed economies help fuel growth
    7. Transport and communication undergo stupendous growth
    8. Reactions against widespread consumerism: anti-Americanism
  C. Communist economies
    1. Five-year plans and sluggish growth
    2. The formation of COMECON
    3. Collectivization of agriculture in Eastern Europe
  D. An urban world
    1. The growth of sprawling suburbs
    2. Refurbishment of ancient city centers
  E. The "Green Revolution" in agriculture
    1. Rapid rise in agricultural productivity
    2. Mechanization and fertilizers
    3. Consolidation of plots into large, efficient farms
    4. A new problem: regular agricultural surpluses
    5. Similar processes at work in the Eastern bloc
  F. Demographic changes
    1. The baby boom of the post-war years
    2. A huge expansion of educational systems
    3. Considerable differentials in the distribution of wealth

V. Cold War crises
  A. The climate of "nuclear terror"
  B. The Korean War
    1. Invasion from the north (1950)
    2. U.S. (and United Nations) intervention
  C. Stirrings in Eastern Europe
    1. Berlin riots of 1953
    2. Gomulka's reforms in Poland (1956)

3.   The Hungarian Revolution of 1956
4.   The "new class" in Yugoslavia
D.   Superpower tensions
1.   The "thaw" of 1955, and "peaceful coexistence"
2.   Sputnik and the Soviet ICBM capability (1957)
3.   The U-2 incident (1960)
4.   The Berlin Wall (1961)
5.   Cuban Missile Crisis (1962)
6.   An accelerating arms race
7.   The global reach of Cold War rivalries
E.   Sino-Soviet rivalry
1.   Mao and the cult of personality in China after 1949
2.   Growing tensions between the two Communist giants
F.   The Brezhnev era
1.   Khrushchev deposed in 1964
2.   Brezhnev presides over Communist orthodoxy
G.   The Cold War as a defining feature of post-war history

Suggestions for Lecture Topics

For a lecture on the Nuremberg trials, see the interesting new book by Joseph Persico, *Nuremberg: Infamy on Trial*. I have found that this subject, when cast as a set of moral questions regarding the gradations of culpability for Nazi war crimes, tends to draw in even the most shy or passive of students; thus, it provides an excellent opportunity for a part-lecture, part-discussion format.

Intellectual currents such as existentialism tend to puzzle a majority of students, unless they are somehow grounded in a specific set of readings. My favorite for this purpose is Camus' *The Plague*. A lecture situating this novel within its broader historical context can effectively precede a class discussion in which the students debate the nuances and meanings of this remarkable literary work.

To accompany a lecture on the European Community (today European Union), an instructor can easily request a host of free films from the Union's liaison office in Washington, D.C. These films cover everything from historical aspects of the EC's development to biographies of its chief architects, like Jean Monnet. Some of the films, such as *Europe: Why?* are clearly designed by the EC's information office to explain to young Europeans how the complex bureaucracy of the European Union works, and why this institution matters in their lives. The film thus becomes a fascinating "primary source document" on the self-presentation of a supranational agency to its constituencies. Students can then pose critical questions about the processes by which a higher "European" identity is being sought by the Euro-crats in Brussels, Luxembourg City, and Strasbourg.

The film *The Battle of Algiers*, by Gilles Pontecorvo, makes an excellent accompaniment to any discussion of decolonization. Students can be encouraged to ask whether the film is "biased." This can then lead into vigorous debates about the deeper ramifications of colonialism and decolonization themselves.

For a lecture on life in the Soviet satellite countries, see the vivid portrayals by Václav Havel in his magnificent essay, "The Power of the Powerless," in Jan Ladislav, ed., *Living in Truth*; the novel by Milan Kundera, *The Unbearable Lightness of Being*; and the essay by Nobel prize-winning poet Czeslaw Milosz, *The Captive Mind*.

Multiple-Choice Questions

1. Control over Germany after World War II was exercised by
   a. Britain, France, Italy, and the United States.
   b. Britain, France, the Soviet Union, and the United States.
   c. Britain, Poland, Denmark, and Holland.
   d. the Soviet Union and the United States.
   e. none of the above

Answer: b

2. The Dumbarton Oaks Conference
   a. paved the way for the invasion of Germany.
   b. paved the way for the creation of the United Nations.
   c. sought to reconcile Roosevelt and Stalin over lend-lease.
   d. set a date for the opening of a second front in Western Europe.
   e. created the European Economic Community.

Answer: b

3. The Truman Doctrine and Marshall Plan were launched in
   a. the same year.
   b. 1946 and 1947.
   c. 1945 and 1947.
   d. 1947 and 1948.
   e. none of the above

Answer: a

4. Existentialism rested on
    a.   the philosophical notion that existence is rational.
    b.   the experience of the wartime killing of Jews.
    c.   the notion that human life is irrational, but that God exists.
    d.   the notion that human life is irrational, and no God exists.
    e.   the hope that human life can become rational.
Answer: d

5. Khrushchev's "secret speech" of 1956
    a.   denounced the conspiracy that had led to Stalin's murder.
    b.   announced that he himself would henceforth take the helm of the
         party.
    c.   denounced the crimes committed by Stalin and his regime.
    d.   denounced the chronic underproduction of Soviet agriculture.
    e.   none of the above
Answer: c

6. Ho Chi Minh was
    a.   a nationalist.
    b.   a Communist.
    c.   a capitalist.
    d.   a trade unionist.
    e.   both a and b
Answer: e

7. The "Green Revolution" was
    a.   a movement to build parks in Europe's cities.
    b.   another name for the environmental movement.
    c.   a massive increase in agricultural production.
    d.   a peaceful takeover of power under Gomulka in Hungary.
    e.   a peaceful takeover of power under Gomulka in Poland.
Answer: c

8. Khrushchev's successor in the U.S.S.R. was
    a.   Malenkov.
    b.   Kosygin.
    c.   Chernenko.
    d.   Beria.
    e.   none of the above
Answer: e

9. Palestine was divided in 1948 into
   a. Israel and Syria.
   b. Israel and Gaza.
   c. Jordan and Jerusalem.
   d. Jordan and Israel.
   e. Suez and the Golan Heights.

Answer: d

10. The decolonization of India resulted in which two new nation-states?
    a. Hindu India and Communist Pakistan
    b. Sikh India and Hindu Pakistan
    c. Hindu India and Buddhist Bangladesh
    d. Muslim India and Hindu Bangladesh
    e. Hindu India and Muslim Pakistan

Answer: e

Short-Answer Questions

1. What were the main reasons for Labour's victory in the British elections of 1945?
2. What were some of the most salient differences between the decolonization of the British Empire and that of the French Empire?
3. What were the main reasons for the "economic miracles" of many Western European nations during the 1950s?
4. What were the principal causes of the Cold War? Explain.
5. Describe the most salient trends that characterized the history of the Soviet Union in the two decades after 1945.

True/False Questions

1. The Potsdam Conference set the principal terms for the capitulation of Italy.

Answer: F

2. Cinema became one of the chief media of post-war art in Europe.

Answer: T

3. Yugoslav communism under Tito followed closely on the model set by the Soviet Union.

Answer: F

4. Josef Stalin died in 1949.

Answer: F

5. The first president of the French Fifth Republic was Charles de Gaulle.

Answer: T

6. Germany and Japan possessed the two fastest-growing economies of the post-war era.

Answer: T

7. The Suez Canal crisis became a major foreign-policy success for Britain and France.

Answer: F

8. Most economists agree that the influence of the Marshall Plan was very limited.

Answer: F

9. The Korean War was fought by the United States and its anti-Communist allies under the auspices of the United Nations.

Answer: T

10. The U.S.S.R. and China, despite their common Communist leadership, became hostile nations in the 1950s.

Answer: T

Chronology

Place the following items in correct chronological order.
1. Dumbarton Oaks Conference
8. Soviets crush Hungarian Revolution against Communist rule
2. Labour victory in Britain
6. Conservatives oust Attlee in Britain
4. Communist coup in Czechoslovakia

   5. Soviet Union acquires atomic bomb
 10. Algeria gains independence
   7. French defeat at Dien Bien Phu
   9. Berlin Wall built
   3. Truman Doctrine and Marshall Plan

Chapter 30
The Emergence of Contemporary Europe and the Collapse of Communism

This chapter describes the main currents of European history since the late 1960s, from the protest movements of the 1960s counterculture to the Revolutions of 1989, from détente to the end of the Cold War.

Chapter Outline

I.   Politics in a changing Western world
    A.   The events of May 1968 in France
        1.   Daniel Cohn-Bendit and French student protests
        2.   French working class supports students
        3.   The victory of De Gaulle's government
        4.   De Gaulle's retirement
    B.   Shifts in Western European politics
        1.   Willy Brandt's "opening toward the East" in Germany
        2.   Helmut Kohl's long dominance in Germany
        3.   Economic struggles of the 1970s Labour governments in Britain
        4.   The "Thatcher Revolution" in Britain
        5.   Mitterand in power in France (1981), followed by Chirac's election (1995)
        6.   Political instability in Italy
        7.   Environmentalists organize Green political parties
    C.   The transition to democracy in Southern Europe
        1.   From dictatorship to democracy in Greece
        2.   Salazar's authoritarian rule ends in 1974 in Portugal
        3.   Opposition to Franco's regime in Spain mounts during 1960s
        4.   Franco's death in 1975, and the accession of a democratic king
    D.   Catholicism in modern Europe

        1.   Declining attendance at Mass

        2.   The liberal currents and the role of Pope John XXIII

        3.   Pope John Paul II's mixture of conservatism and activism

   E.   The European Community and the European Union

        1.   Britain, Denmark, and Ireland join in 1973

        2.   Decline in tariff barriers

        3.   The Treaty of Maastricht (1992)

        4.   Ambivalence toward supranational institutions among European populations

II.   Economic growth and limits

   A.   Prosperity and mass culture

        1.   Growth in mass communications

        2.   American consumerism spreads through Europe

        3.   Burgeoning tourism

        4.   Paid vacations for the working class

   B.   Oil and the global economy

        1.   Wars in the Middle East result in higher oil prices

        2.   Economic impact of the OPEC oil embargo of the 1970s

   C.   Changing contours of economic life

        1.   Shrinking role of peasant farmers

        2.   Growing power of women in the workforce

        3.   Large influx of foreign "guest workers"

        4.   Rising violence and xenophobia against foreigners

III.   Threats to peace

   A.   Nuclear weapons

        1.   Détente and arms talks between the superpowers

        2.   The Soviet invasion of Afghanistan (1979)

        3.   Renewed Cold War in the 1980s

   B.   Terrorism

        1.   Frustrated extremists on left and right take to violent means

        2.   Italian terrorists threaten stability of the Italian Republic

        3.   Arab and Islamic terrorism

   C.   Religious and ethnic divisions

        1.   Religious strife in Northern Ireland

        2.   Separatism movements in Britain, France, and Spain

        3.   Serb-Croat tensions and other rivalries in Yugoslavia

        4.   Other lines of conflict in Eastern Europe

IV. The fall of communism

A. Eastern Europe and the Soviet shadow
    1. Dubček and the Prague Spring in Czechoslovakia
    2. The "Brezhnev Doctrine"
    3. Solidarity in Poland (1980–1981)
    4. Orthodoxy in East Germany, Bulgaria, post-1968 Czechoslovakia
    5. Economic experimentation in Hungary
    6. "National Communism" under Ceausescu in Romania
B. The Gorbachev era
    1. A succession of gerontocrats
    2. Gorbachev's rise to power (1985)
    3. *Glasnost*, or "openness" in public affairs
    4. *Perestroika*, or "restructuring" in the economy
    5. The Congress of People's Deputies (1988)
C. Factors that contributed to the fall of communism
    1. Nationalist sentiments among the subject peoples of the U.S.S.R.
    2. An assertive democratic opposition, born under Gorbachev
    3. A worsening economic crisis
    4. Dramatic changes in foreign policy, ending the Cold War
    5. A key factor in demands for reform in Eastern Europe:
        Gorbachev's ending of the Brezhnev Doctrine
D. Poland and Hungary
    1. An organized opposition forms in Poland and Hungary
    2. Free elections in Hungary (summer 1989) weaken Communists
    3. Economic crisis in Poland causes return of Solidarity
    4. Sweeping electoral victory for Solidarity's candidates
    5. Polish and Hungarian Communists change their name and
        approach
E. The collapse of the Berlin Wall and East German communism
    1. The flight of East Germans into Hungary (1989)
    2. Honecker's desperate bid to control the shifting situation
    3. Soviet support for reformists in East Germany
    4. Communist reformer Egon Krenz opens the East-West barriers
    5. Edging toward closer cooperation between the two Germanys
    6. Reunification (October 3, 1990) of Germanys
F. "Velvet Revolution" in Czechoslovakia
    1. Ten days that swept away a dictatorship
    2. Václav Havel and Civic Forum
    3. Utter rejection of socialism by the population
    4. Havel becomes the new president in December 1989
    5. Problems between Czechs and Slovaks, leading to a split in 1993

G. Revolutions in Bulgaria, Romania, and Albania
1. Bulgaria's Zhivkov resigns in November 1989
2. Attempts to foment anti-Turkish hatred in Bulgaria
3. Romania: the one bloody exception amid the Revolutions of 1989
4. Ceausescu's cult of the leader
5. The showdown in Timisoara
6. Ceausescu unleashes security police against demonstrators
7. Ceausescu's execution (December 25, 1989)
8. Ion Iliescu, a reformist Communist, elected in 1990
9. Albanians join the international movement against communism
H. The collapse of the Soviet Union
1. Stirrings of discontent spread through the U.S.S.R.
2. Nationalism within the Russian Republic
3. Lithuania unilaterally declares independence (1990)
4. The resignation of Eduard Shevardnadze
5. Yeltsin urges more radical reforms
6. Gorbachev loses control of the movement he had unleashed
7. The attempted hard-liner coup of August 1991
8. Yeltsin seizes the helm
9. A string of declarations of independence by former republics
10. Gorbachev resigns (December 25, 1991)
I. The disintegration of Yugoslavia
1. Reassertion of Serb nationalism under Slobodan Milošević
2. Slovenia's secession (June 1991)
3. Croats and Serbs at war (1991)
4. Civil war within Bosnia; Bosnian Serbs conquer large territory
5. U.N. peacekeepers face frustrating task
6. Dangers of international escalation
J. Challenges of the post-Communist world
1. The high stakes of a peaceful transition to democracy in Russia
2. Strong nationalist trends among Eastern Europeans
3. Reformist Communist parties show strength in Balkans
4. The trials of transition to market economies
5. Ethnic tensions resurgent in Eastern Europe
6. Conflicts among former Soviet peoples

V. Conclusion
A. The reduction of Europe's influence over the rest of the world
B. Dangers of nuclear proliferation

  C. Prospects of "ecocide" in former Communist lands
  D. Seeking a new role for NATO and the European Union
  E. The powder keg of immigration
      1. Rising intolerance, racism, and xenophobia
      2. Aggressive nationalism in Russia and the Balkans

Suggestions for Lecture Topics

For a lecture on the May 1968 events in France, see Keith Reader, ed., *May 1968 in France.*

On the Thatcher Revolution in Britain, see Peter Jenkins, *Mrs. Thatcher's Revolution.*

Most undergraduate students are fascinated by the intellectual problem of identifying the causes of the Revolutions of 1989; a lecture on this topic should take into account the thesis advanced by some conservatives that the end of the Cold War marked the triumph of President Ronald Reagan's vast military buildup of the 1980s. Two accounts that shed considerable light on this and other key issues bearing on the Revolutions of 1989 are David Remnick, *Lenin's Tomb,* and Gale Stokes, *The Walls Came Tumbling Down.*

On the Yugoslavian catastrophe see Misha Glenny, *The Fall of Yugoslavia.*

On the history and changing roles of the United Nations, see Adam Roberts and Benedict Kingsbury, eds., *United Nations, Divided World.*

Multiple-Choice Questions

  1. Daniel Cohn-Bendit was
      a. the Czechoslovakian ambassador to the Soviet Union during the Velvet Revolution.
      b. a leader of the French student uprising in May 1968.
      c. the German foreign minister who oversaw the process of reunification.
      d. Dubček's right-hand man during the Prague Spring.
      e. none of the above

Answer: b

  2. Charles De Gaulle
      a. resigned amid the upheaval of May 1968.
      b. was forced to resign after an East German spy was found working in his entourage.

    c.   died suddenly in 1969 while in office.
    d.   was assassinated by right-wingers who opposed his Algerian policy.
    e.   resigned in 1969 after a referendum that he supported was rejected by the French electorate.

Answer: e

3. Terrorism in Europe during the 1970s was carried out by
    a.   right-wingers seeking to bring about the imposition of authoritarian rule, as well as left-wingers seeking to destabilize democratic institutions.
    b.   Palestinians seeking to publicize their plight and their cause.
    c.   regional separatists in various European nations.
    d.   a and b but not c
    e.   all of the above

Answer: e

4. The Treaty of Maastricht
    a.   sought to broker an agreement between East and West Germany.
    b.   was the founding document of superpower détente during the 1970s.
    c.   paved the way for a reduction of conflict in Northern Ireland.
    d.   set target levels for further reductions in national barriers within the European Union.
    e.   none of the above

Answer: d

5. *Glasnost* means
    a.   flexibility.
    b.   openness.
    c.   courage.
    d.   rejection of corruption.
    e.   fairness.

Answer: b

6. The first signs of the Revolutions of 1989 appeared in
    a.   Poland and Czechoslovakia.
    b.   Hungary and Romania.
    c.   Romania and Bulgaria.
    d.   East Germany and Poland.
    e.   Poland and Hungary.

Answer: e

7. Mikhail Gorbachev
   a. was a Communist who believed that communism needed reform in order to survive.
   b. was a former Communist who believed that only a change into full-fledged capitalism would allow his country to survive.
   c. only embarked on his reforms under pressure from the military and K.G.B.
   d. strongly believed that the U.S.S.R. should be broken up into smaller units.
   e. felt that Boris Yeltsin was too conservative for the times.

Answer: a

8. Václav Havel was
   a. a playwright.
   b. an electrician.
   c. a trade unionist.
   d. a musician.
   e. none of the above

Answer: a

9. The first Soviet territory to declare its independence was
   a. Georgia.
   b. Azerbaijan.
   c. Latvia.
   d. Lithuania.
   e. Ukraine.

Answer: d

10. Bosnia's population is primarily made up of
    a. Serbs and Croats, some of them Christians, some of them Muslims.
    b. Slavs, Germans, and Macedonians, most of them Christians.
    c. Ethnic Albanians, Serbs, Slovenians, and Dalmatians, some of them Christians, some of them Muslims.
    d. Mostly Croatian Muslims.
    e. Ruthenians, Croats, Serbs, and some Hungarians, most of them Christians.

Answer: a

Short-Answer Questions

1. What were the main goals of the rebelling students during the May 1968 upheaval in France?
2. Would you describe the unification process among Western European nations as having failed? Explain.
3. What were the principal causes of the Revolutions of 1989?
4. Why was Romania the only nation to experience major bloodshed in the Revolutions of 1989? Why did other Eastern European nations escape this ugly fate?
5. What were the principal causes for the disintegration of Yugoslavia?

True/False Questions

1. Timisoara was the site of a Russian massacre in Lithuania.

Answer: F

2. Willy Brandt sought to relax tensions with the Eastern bloc countries.

Answer: T

3. Helmut Kohl, Margaret Thatcher, and François Mitterrand were conservatives who held office for unusually long terms.

Answer: F

4. Pope John XXIII brought about reforms in the Catholic Church.

Answer: T

5. The Brezhnev Doctrine stated that Communist states would intervene militarily to help maintain Communist regimes wherever they appeared to be threatened.

Answer: T

6. Gorbachev repealed the Brezhnev Doctrine.

Answer: T

7. *Perestroika* was the name of Gorbachev's reformist political party.

Answer: F

8. The Albanian Communist regime sought to foment anti-Turkish sentiment as a way of deflecting criticisms of the government.

Answer: F

9. Eduard Shevardnadze was one of Gorbachev's allies.

Answer: T

10. Slobodan Milošević became famous for insisting that his army observe the human rights of its opponents.

Answer: F

Chronology

Place the following items in correct chronological order.
- 2. Britain joins EC
- 4. Soviet invasion of Afghanistan
- 6. Falklands War
- 5. Solidarity union formed in Poland
- 1. May uprising in Paris
- 10. Treaty of Maastricht
- 7. Mikhail Gorbachev becomes Soviet leader
- 9. Reunification of Germany
- 8. Death of Nicolae Ceausescu
- 3. Death of Francisco Franco

INSTRUCTOR'S MANUAL AND TEST-ITEM FILE

Merriman's
A HISTORY OF MODERN EUROPE
by Michael Bess
Vanderbilt University

The *Instructor's Manual and Test-Item File* accompanying John Merriman's new text, *A History of Modern Europe,* provides instructors invaluable help in creating and organizing lectures and short-answer exams. For each text chapter this manual provides a detailed outline, a series of potential lecture topics, and a number of effective short-answer questions.

The 1,000 questions in the *Instructor's Manual and Test-Item File* are also available separately in electronic form on the Norton TestMaker system. This software features easy-to-use pull-down menus, a flexible system for adding, scrambling, or modifying questions, and a powerful grade-management system.

This ancillary is available free to instructors who adopt a minimum number of copies of *A History of Modern Europe.*

Cover illustration: *The Harbour of Middelburg* by Adriaen van der Venne. Rijksmuseum, Amsterdam.

W·W·NORTON

NEW YORK · LONDON

ISBN 0-393-96887-1

9 780393 968873

90000